D0454049

"Parents and practitioners alike will greatly e
from *The Holistic Baby Guide*. Neustaedter's
recommendations are well-researched and comp.......
practical and accessible. He provides natural solutions that utilize
the best of integrative medicine for treating the most common,
vexing problems of infancy. Parents who follow his guidelines are
very likely to have healthier, happier babies; practitioners who
recommend his book will know they've done a great service for
their patients."

—Janet Levatin, MD, board-certified pediatrician and
clinical instructor in pediatrics, Harvard University

"Neustaedter has given us a unique perspective on the common
problems in early childhood that is at once comprehensive and
holistic. His voice will be a welcome relief to worried parents
and a wonderful resource to practitioners seeking alternatives to
conventional pediatric interventions."

—Stephen Cowan, MD, FAAP, founder of the Holistic
Developmental Center for Children

WITHDRAWN

the holistic baby guide

Alternative Care for Common Health Problems

RANDALL NEUSTAEDTER, OMD

New Harbinger Publications, Inc.

Publisher's Note

Care has been taken to confirm the accuracy of the information presented and to describe generally accepted practices. However, the authors, editors, and publisher are not responsible for errors or omissions or for any consequences from application of the information in this book and make no warranty, express or implied, with respect to the contents of the publication.

The authors, editors, and publisher have exerted every effort to ensure that any drug selection and dosage set forth in this text are in accordance with current recommendations and practice at the time of publication. However, in view of ongoing research, changes in government regulations, and the constant flow of information relating to drug therapy and drug reactions, the reader is urged to check the package insert for each drug for any change in indications and dosage and for added warnings and precautions. This is particularly important when the recommended agent is a new or infrequently employed drug.

Some drugs and medical devices presented in this publication may have Food and Drug Administration (FDA) clearance for limited use in restricted research settings. It is the responsibility of the health care provider to ascertain the FDA status of each drug or device planned for use in their clinical practice.

Distributed in Canada by Raincoast Books

Copyright © 2010 by Randall Neustaedter
New Harbinger Publications, Inc.
5674 Shattuck Avenue
Oakland, CA 94609
www.newharbinger.com

Cover design by Amy Shoup; Text design by Amy Shoup and Michele Waters-Kermes; Acquired by Catharine Sutker

All Rights Reserved. Printed in the United States of America.

Library of Congress Cataloging-in-Publication Data

Neustaedter, Randall, 1949-
    The holistic baby guide : alternative care for common health problems / Randall Neustaedter.
        p. cm.
    Includes bibliographical references and index.
    ISBN-13: 978-1-57224-693-5 (pbk. : alk. paper)
    ISBN-10: 1-57224-693-6 (pbk. : alk. paper)   1. Pediatrics--Popular works.   2.   Children--
Diseases--Alternative treatment--Popular works.   3.   Holistic medicine--Popular works.   I. Title.
    RJ61.N388 2010
    618.92--dc22

                                    2009044367

12   11   10

10   9   8   7   6   5   4   3   2   1   First printing

contents

----

introduction

The Holistic Baby Guide is designed to give you, as a parent, the tools you need to solve the most common health problems encountered during a baby's first year. If you have a toddler, then most of this information will apply to her as well. For new parents who are intent on creating the best emotional and physical environment for their baby, the onset of symptoms can be very distressing. Unfortunately, soon after parents settle in with their new baby and get siblings adjusted to the new addition, life often becomes disrupted by the baby's discomfort in the form of crying episodes. A new baby is vulnerable and completely dependent on her parents. A screaming baby in discomfort or a baby who develops patterns of recurrent illness represents one of the first challenges for a new parent. The most common health problems of infants are digestive disturbances, skin problems, and chronic respiratory congestion with infections and allergies. This book is dedicated to solving these problems using a holistic approach because conventional pediatrics has relatively few effective treatments for these very frequently encountered symptoms. For their baby's problems, parents are usually offered medications with recognized toxicity (acid blockers for reflux, steroids for skin problems, and antibiotics for acute illnesses). None of these drugs are ideal, some are ineffective, and some cause more problems than they cure.

a more natural path

A holistic pediatric approach to the common health problems of babies offers alternative strategies that are safe and effective. There are many natural measures that you can use to help your baby's symptoms, and holistic pediatric care provides curative medical treatment for these conditions without producing unwanted and harmful side effects. In fact, treating babies with holistic methods during the first year of life offers a curative program that can prevent chronic problems throughout childhood. In *The Holistic Baby Guide* I will describe the treatment plan that you need to feel confident about managing your baby's health problems. You will learn methods to prevent the onset of symptoms, home measures to relieve symptoms, and treatments you can expect from holistic medical care that will solve your baby's recurrent health problems.

Unless you are already consulting a holistic practitioner, you will notice a dramatic difference between the information contained in this book and what you are told by your pediatrician. The underlying principles of this book are founded in the sciences of homeopathic medicine, Chinese medicine, modern functional medicine, and chiropractic medicine. The integration of these sciences forms the backbone of holistic pediatrics.

A Variety of Sciences

Homeopathic medicine is based on the understanding that the body has the innate ability to heal if given the proper stimulus to move in the right direction. This is accomplished by taking the proper homeopathic medicine prescribed for the person's complex of symptoms. The stimulus is energetic in nature and depends on the vitality of the body's healing mechanisms. The unique method of preparing homeopathic medicines creates a dynamic potency that differs from the effects of herbal medicines. A homeopathic medicine initiates a deep healing process, enabling even a single dose of a medicine to persist for months. Homeopathy works especially well in children because of their resilience and their ability to respond quickly to treatment.

Over the past three thousand years, *Chinese medicine* has developed a sophisticated understanding of the energetic balance in the body. This balance includes the interactions of different body systems, especially the respiratory, digestive, and nervous systems. And these functions can be easily upset in infants. An imbalance in these systems can often be corrected simply by administering the proper formula of Chinese herbs. Babies are simple and uncorrupted by past treatment, and their imbalances are usually very amenable to correction with a minimal amount of treatment.

Functional medicine is a modern scientific system for understanding physiological processes, primarily through laboratory testing and prescribing herbal and nutritional products based on this understanding of individual needs. The integration of medical models that promote healing provides a powerful system that addresses the causes of imbalance in the body. Addressing the underlying cause of illness using a holistic approach will always result in a better outcome than using only treatment directed at individual symptoms.

Chiropractic medicine primarily concerns itself with structural problems in the spine, which will place strain and tension on spinal nerves and connective tissues as well as on internal organs supplied by these nerves. This imbalance, often referred to as vertebral subluxations, can result in nerve irritation, inflammation, and dysfunction in the areas supplied by these nerves. Treatment involves adjustment of the spine, the bones of the skull, and other bones and joints of the body to restore healthy function in the surrounding and associated connective tissue, muscles, and organs. In addition, many chiropractors take a holistic view of the body, which may include nutritional and lifestyle adjustments to maintain health. Chiropractic is especially useful in babies because the torsion and pressure exerted on the infant's body during the birthing process can result in spinal and cranial misalignment, which can be corrected using the manual techniques of chiropractic adjustments.

benefits of holistic pediatrics

Holistic pediatrics represents cutting-edge science that treats illness in children with an inclusive perspective, addressing genetic predispositions, the underlying causes of imbalance, and the symptoms themselves with nontoxic therapies. This is a system that can address most common health problems in children, providing solutions for parents that consist of reliable and safe treatment. And the methods can often be carried out by parents themselves when they have the right information. In this book I provide that information for parents. Holistic pediatric methods are safe, gentle, and curative. Their goal is to relieve symptoms and correct the body's imbalances, bringing the baby's system into a more harmonious state of health. This book is about managing health problems. To learn the essential information you need about parenting methods and raising children with a natural lifestyle, I suggest you also read my book *Child Health Guide: Holistic Pediatrics for Parents* (Neustaedter 2005).

what this book offers

The Holistic Baby Guide describes home measures, lifestyle interventions, dietary practices, nutritional supplements, and holistic medical approaches that can solve many of your baby's health problems, giving symptomatic relief and strengthening immune function to both overcome acute illness and solve persistent health problems. The book consistently empowers you to resolve the worrisome health issues that you confront during the first year of your baby's life. Here I will describe preventive and curative practices that will maintain a healthy, vital, and robust immune system.

Each chapter in *The Holistic Baby Guide* addresses a particular problem or system of the body. We will start with the digestive problems of infants because this is the first body system that is stressed, and the digestive tract is usually where symptoms of imbalance first appear. A baby's digestive system is particularly vulnerable because from day one she encounters food that requires digestion, and your baby may not always manage the daily grind of eating, burping, and pooping with the efficiency that nature requires for her to be symptom free. The second chapter of the book focuses on the skin. Your baby's beautiful and tender skin is where any immune imbalances will first appear externally. Persistent or recurrent rashes, eczema, and baby acne are all signs that something is wrong with a baby's inner ecology.

By five or six months of age, protective maternal antibodies start to dissipate and most babies start to become susceptible to viruses in the environment. I have dedicated two chapters of this book to fevers and acute illnesses, discussing the home measures you can apply to help remedy these problems and the holistic medical interventions that can solve them without the use of drugs. As discussed in this book and in common medical usage, *acute illness* refers to a self-limited infection or set of symptoms that will naturally end in some amount of time (like a cold, bronchitis, or teething). *Chronic illness* usually refers to a set of symptoms or a diagnostic category that persists over a long period of time, possibly indefinitely (such as allergies or asthma). Several chapters cover more complicated recurrent symptoms of the respiratory tract, ear problems, persistent sinusitis, and asthma. You can use the information in these chapters for problems that may develop in infancy and continue into the toddler years. What you learn here will even be viable if these types of symptoms develop in the preschool years and persist into later childhood.

In the final chapter, I provide a general overview of immune function and discuss the immune-system imbalances and weaknesses that are so common in today's babies and toddlers. These common imbalances result in repeated illnesses and chronic allergies. This chapter integrates the holistic methods covered in preceding chapters, describing a plan for boosting and rebalancing the immune system and preventing recurrent illness.

Today's babies are plagued with chronic health problems at an unprecedented rate. Repeated ear infections, eczema, asthma, and chronic congestion from allergies and sinusitis are rampant problems that never existed at these rates in the past. All of these symptoms occur as a result of an immune system imbalance in today's children. These problems can and should be cured through proper diet, nutritional support, and appropriate holistic medical care. In chapter 8, I will share methods for rebalancing and building immune function in your baby or toddler.

the research

The information contained in *The Holistic Baby Guide* is based on the cumulative experience of the holistic pediatric community of providers and my experience treating babies for over thirty years. The nutritional information is based on scientific inquiry. Conventional medicine tends to honor data and treatment protocols verified by controlled clinical trials. The gold standard is a clinical study that includes two groups of patients. A *placebo control group* is compared to a similar *treatment group* (the subjects in the study who are receiving the treatment being examined). This comparison is done in what is called a *randomized approach*, which means that the subjects are chosen at random to receive treatment or placebo. Both groups are controlled for other possible contributing factors that may influence their outcomes so that both groups are as similar as possible. That is, the groups are examined to determine whether anything other than the experimental treatment may be affecting the results.

This type of study is expensive and often only possible with a single intervention—only one treatment can be studied at a time. In the real world of pediatrics, most conventional treatments are based on what doctors have seen work in their practice, on tradition, and on hearsay (what the pediatrician's colleagues do), not on clinical studies. Whenever possible, I make reference in the text to scientific clinical studies. However, holistic methods often are not based on studies like these because many of the guidelines for treatment predate the invention of these types of studies or because such a study is impractical.

The holistic medical approaches I describe in this book, including herbal therapy and homeopathy, are based on hundreds or even thousands of years of empirical practice and hundreds of textbooks of holistic pediatric principles. I also rely on my thirty years of practice as a holistic practitioner. I and other holistic pediatric practitioners have synthesized these practices into a consistent and reliable system of child health care, and my aim in writing this book is to make these forms of treatment and preventive maintenance accessible to parents. Armed with this information, you can apply the principles yourself and also seek out the appropriate medical care to solve the common health problems of infancy before they become chronic and persistent illness and disease.

----

who this book is for: parents and practitioners

I assume *The Holistic Baby Guide*, like many parenting books, will be read by practitioners as well as parents. Frankly, parenting books are easier to read than medical texts and a lot easier to understand, and doctors like an easy read as much as anyone. I have summarized studies, and I often review highly technical data in a way that I hope is not too tedious. This book contains many protocols for understanding and treating pediatric medical conditions (with specifics available in the appendices), and the information is presented in much the same way that we teach pediatricians and other holistic pediatric practitioners. In my experience, parents appreciate information, explanations, and evidence that will help them make an informed decision and feel confident about the medical decisions they make. My hope is that this book will assist new parents and even seasoned pediatric practitioners to make the first year of babies' lives healthy and free of medical problems, setting the stage for a lifetime of good health.

CHAPTER 1

- - - - - - - - - -

holistic pediatrics:
an overview

This book describes medical care and parenting advice from the perspective of holistic pediatrics. This growing field of specialization encompasses a wide range of principles and philosophies derived from a multitude of sources. Holistic pediatrics tends to be inclusive rather than restrictive and integrative rather than exclusionary. Many types of practitioners utilize holistic pediatric principles, including pediatricians, naturopathic physicians, acupuncturists, chiropractors, and others. A professional organization, the Holistic Pediatric Association, exists to educate, inform, and unite the practitioners and parents who use these methods. Several organizations exist to train practitioners in these methods. And many books describe the integrative treatments and perspectives of holistic pediatrics. (See appendix 2 for details on many of these.)

the building blocks of holistic pediatrics

The principles of holistic pediatrics are inclusive of many philosophies, including Chinese medicine, homeopathic medicine, herbal medicine, chiropractic medicine, and many other approaches that emphasize natural means of healing. These methods comprise the fundamental systems of healing described in this book, and I've applied them to the health problems I discuss. A holistic approach to children must include attention to their physical, emotional, developmental, and spiritual well-being, all of which are interdependent. In this sense, holistic pediatrics is really a way of *caring* for children rather than merely *treating* them. Children require nurturing care, and this is especially true when there are problems that cause suffering. Whenever possible, a holistic approach will avoid treatments that have potential side effects or dangers, favoring gentle methods that stimulate the body's own healing processes and correct imbalances. At the same time, "holism" implies that a view of the whole child is considered, even when the focus is on a specific symptom or condition. A holistic or integrated method will consider the broader issues that underlie a problem and the ramifications of the symptoms on other body functions. A holistic view seeks the cause of symptoms and also focuses on the prevention of recurrences and achieving a complete cure (the permanent eradication of symptoms). By contrast, conventional medicine tends to focus on temporary relief of a symptom for a limited amount of time. Of course, many conventional pediatricians and pediatric specialists look for causes and promote a preventive approach to children's medical problems. Holistic pediatrics just tends to be more inclusive and looks to deeper levels of imbalance.

A holistic approach will usually consider nutrition first, since food provides the building blocks of healing. A healthy diet during pregnancy will promote a strong and resilient baby. And when your infant receives healthy nutrition, his immune system is more likely to be balanced and resistant to infections. The concept of using whole, natural foods free of pesticides and other petroleum products and additives serves as a foundation for a healthy child. My book *Child Health Guide: Holistic Pediatrics for Parents* describes many of the general nutritional aspects of children's care, and I'll be describing some nutritional approaches that affect the health problems covered in this book in later chapters. A holistic approach also seeks to avoid any aggravating influences on health problems, including harmful foods, environmental exposure, toxic chemicals in household products, and medications with side effects.

Balance and Energy

Holistic care of children uses methods that assist healing without causing unwanted side effects. Therefore, it may incorporate any medical model that promotes a healing response, especially those that work at deep energetic levels of the body. By energy I mean the animating and vital forces that precede chemical or physiologic changes. Homeopathy incorporates the concept of vital energy to portray the body's innate ability to heal. The vitality can be weakened by many factors, including stress and disease processes. Chinese medicine defines several categories of this vitality, including Prenatal Qi, which precedes birth and is inherited from the baby's mother, and different types of Postnatal Qi, derived from food, air, and the body's own digestive and respiratory processes.

The most profound therapeutic changes in the body occur when an intervention stimulates an energetic response prior to chemical changes. This means that some therapies are capable of initiating responses at the level of vital function, at the animating and nutritive levels of the body. Both homeopathy and Chinese herbal formulas, as well as physical approaches that affect the body's energetic pathways (such as chiropractic, Reiki, and osteopathic adjustments), are able to stimulate health at these primary levels. These medical systems have no side effects because they are eliciting responses in the body, offering a stimulus for the body's own best defenses. Homeopathic medicines are energetic in nature. They do not contain any active chemical ingredients, and they will directly act on the body's own vital force. Herbal medicines do contain active ingredients, but they also provide energy from living organisms (plants and some animal products) that directly effect specific energetic pathways in the body. Chiropractic and other physical forms of treatment can also provide a strong stimulus to heal and induce a new physical and energetic balance in the body. These are all medical systems that use a physical intervention to affect the energetic level of the body. There may also be resultant chemical effects in body tissues, but the reanimating and rebalancing effect at an energetic level is integral to their success. The changes in specific forms of energy flow and energy balance in the body accounts for the preventive and curative effect of these methods. Of course, it is also beneficial to provide the body with the nutrients it needs for healing, and in babies this may take the form of nutritional supplements. There are also times when conventional drugs or surgery may be needed as part of an overall holistic plan. But integrating these with other healing interventions will also address the underlying imbalances at the root of the symptoms.

A Whole-Body Approach

Even when the focus of a treatment plan is directed at a single symptom, a holistic perspective will take into consideration factors that may be contributing to the causes that exist at other levels. Conventional pediatrics has a tendency to look at isolated symptoms disconnected from each other, as if the body were a machine composed of disparate parts rather than an integrated whole. A holistic approach considers how all physical and energetic systems of the body are interconnected. For example, a baby may come to the doctor because of a skin rash, but a holistic approach will prompt the doctor to consider problems in other areas of the body that may be affecting the skin. So instead of simply sending the parent and infant home with a topical cream for the rash, the holistic practitioner will consider whether the baby may have digestive problems that underlie and cause an immune dysfunction. The skin ailment may be a symptom of a larger issue, so the doctor would suggest treatment for the troubling rash but also consider treating the baby's digestive imbalance.

Babies are also intimately connected to their mothers. Her state of health during pregnancy and lactation will directly affect her baby. A holistic view will also include preventive measures during pregnancy and the factors in a breastfeeding mother's diet or intake of chemicals that may be adversely affecting her breastfeeding baby. While we will touch on aspects of holistic prevention, you can find a more exhaustive treatment of the subject in my *Child Health Guide*.

- -

treatment methods

Although there are many possible avenues to pursue for treating your baby from a holistic perspective, there are a few that constitute the backbone of holistic treatment. These are nutritional supplements, homeopathic medicine, and Chinese medicine. There are other methods that I also suggest in this book (including chiropractic care and Western herbs), which you may utilize in certain circumstances. But because of the central role of these therapies in your child's holistic care, it makes sense to spend a little time here making sure the concepts of these therapies are familiar to you. Nutritional support is a familiar idea to our culture and really needs no special explanation, but homeopathy and Chinese medicine may be new systems to you that require a little description.

Homeopathic Medicine

The principles of homeopathy were formulated just two hundred years ago by a German physician, Samuel Hahnemann. Since that time the basic concepts underlying homeopathic treatment have remained the same. Homeopathy involves the prescription of medicines prepared by homeopathic pharmacies from plant, mineral, and animal sources. The decision to use any particular medicine is based only on the symptoms of the individual patient. Prescriptions are not decided because of any theory or diagnosis. The symptoms of the patient are simply matched to the symptoms that are associated with each medicine. The closest match is the correct prescription. The medicines are referred to by the Latin name of the substance prescribed. The poison ivy plant is *Rhus toxicodendron*, potassium bicarbonate is *Kali carbonicum*, and the venom of the honey bee is *Apis mellifica*. Homeopathic medicines forever bear these names in any country. In the original or classical form of homeopathy, only one medicine is prescribed at a time, the one medicine that best fits the symptoms. This is the method described in this book and in most other books about home prescribing. You can find combinations of homeopathic medicines at many health-food stores intended for specific conditions such as sore throats or teething, but these are usually just mixtures of the most commonly used medicines for these conditions. Most homeopaths discourage the use of combination remedies, favoring the method of discovering the one medicine that is most indicated based on the symptoms. Books that explain the use of homeopathic medicines for various health problems will discuss the distinctions between medicines based on a description of symptoms. For example, one medicine might be more appropriate for sharp, excruciating pain and a screaming baby, and another medicine would be prescribed for a clingy, sad baby who is just whimpering. These distinctions are based on the extensive knowledge base from which homeopathic medicines originate and the cumulative past experience of homeopathic practitioners. Because homeopathic medicines are so intimately associated with the symptoms they treat, some texts will also describe the medicine in terms of symptoms. For example, a text might say "the *Pulsatilla* child is sad and needy of attention during an illness, while the *Hepar* child is irritable and touchy at the slightest interference," indicating that the medicine corresponds to a child who acts this way.

Homeopathy came out of a particular historical period in Western medicine and was formulated within a tradition of thinking in medicine at the time known as *vitalism*, a philosophy that holds that the body is propelled by a force that is distinct from biological and chemical reactions. Thus the understanding of homeopathic therapeutics is usually conceived and described within this framework. Homeopathy is known as and acknowledged to be an energetic system of medicine, which means that the medicines are assumed to act at an energetic level of the body. This stimulus to the energetic, animating life force precedes any physiological or chemical effects that the medicine might induce. That principle is the hardest one for Western minds to integrate. In this sense, homeopathy is more similar to other energetic forms of treatment such as Reiki therapy and qigong, Asian systems that purport only to impart and move energy. Homeopathic medicines are prepared in a way that actually eliminates all molecules of the original substance through a process of serial dilutions in alcohol and water. The resulting medicine has no detectable residual molecules of the original source (for example, plant alkaloids). It is therefore thought that the process of homeopathic pharmacy itself imparts a change at a molecular energetic level within the solution of the medicine. This pharmaceutical process sets homeopathy apart from all other herbal therapies, which use the crude herbs themselves.

On the other hand, homeopathic medicine also originated within the culture of Western medicine and homeopathic texts use language and disease description familiar to Western science. Homeopathy is a Western system and has no crossover or common conceptual ties with forms of Asian medicine.

Chinese Medicine

Of all the Asian systems of medicine, Chinese medicine is most familiar and the most disseminated system in America and Europe. Ayurvedic medicine from India, Tibetan medicine, and Korean medicine are all utilized and studied in our cultures, but Chinese medicine has been adopted and integrated within conventional Western medical settings and is licensed as a distinct medical practice in most of the United States. Acupuncturists practice in hospitals and medical centers and function within the legal purview of state medical boards.

Although Chinese medicine in particular and Asian medicines in general are increasingly accepted in the West, their concepts may seem unfamiliar and unusual. Chinese medicine is probably the most highly developed of any Asian medical system and certainly the most thoroughly researched. Chinese medicine grew out of a traditional philosophy and cosmology that is thousands of years old. The concepts of *yin* and *yang* and *Qi* (pronounced "chee") permeate classical Chinese thinking and philosophy as well as traditional chinese medicine.

Chinese medicine is old and its concepts are archaic. They originated in a prescientific era when explanations derived from direct experience viewed from a distinct philosophical perspective. Certain concepts are understood and accepted as axiomatic in Chinese medicine. Qi animates the body and mind. Disease is caused by invasion of Heat, Cold, Wind, Damp, and other pathogenic influences that are converted to these same conditions in the body. The obstructed flow of Qi causes pain. Dampness causes phlegm production. These concepts permeate Chinese medicine and Chinese pediatrics, and treatments are directed at these conditions.

Qi is produced in the body, according to Chinese medical thinking, and it flows between organ systems and through channels or meridians from one body part to another in a connected and interactive array. Herbs can direct and manipulate Qi and resolve pathogenic influences (Heat, Dampness, and so on). *Acupuncture* (the manipulation of points along the channels of energy in the body with needles or massage or other forms of stimulation) can alter the flow of Qi and influence the body's efforts to heal. The organ systems are considered to be functional units that interact and maintain an energetic balance in the body that promotes health. These organ systems are named after physical organs (Heart, Spleen, Lung, Kidney, Liver), but they are understood to be energetic in nature with particular functions. They interact and keep each other nourished and also controlled so that one system does not become overactive. An imbalance in these organ systems results in symptoms and disease. Using herbs, specific diet changes, and acupuncture can alter the balance of these organ systems and also subdue, drain, purge, and eliminate their pathogenic qualities of Heat, Dampness, and so on. Translated into Western terms, herbs can have anti-inflammatory effects (relieving Heat) and decongesting effects (draining Dampness and Phlegm). Herbs can also *tonify* or strengthen specific energetic deficiencies in the organ systems. For example, it is thought that the digestive problems of infants arise primarily from a deficiency of Spleen and Stomach Qi (responsible for digestive function), which can be strengthened with herbs.

It is not necessary for you as a parent to understand the intricacies and complexities of Chinese medical principles, but these concepts are discussed in the context of health problems in each of the following chapters and some familiarity with their origins will be helpful to you. In most cases it will be necessary to consult with an acupuncturist or Chinese herbalist to apply these principles to the treatment of your baby.

----

summary

Holistic care may include many different forms of treatment, and there is usually more than one way to treat a particular ailment or imbalance in your baby. Individual practitioners may have their own specialties and areas of expertise, and you as a parent may choose to develop an integrated or holistic treatment plan for your baby that brings together different therapeutic approaches carried out by different medical professionals. In the following chapters I will usually discuss several possible approaches to an individual health problem, and you can decide what paths to follow in consultation with your baby's health care provider.

The first area in which babies tend to develop health problems is the digestive tract, and that's where we'll start. A healthy digestive system is paramount to maintaining overall health in your baby, so it is appropriate to begin there.

CHAPTER 2

----

digestive problems:
colic and reflux

Your baby is an eating machine. Especially in the first few months of life, eating and digestion occupy inordinate amounts of time. Digesting food is taxing on an infant's system, and many symptoms and health problems during the first year have their origin in the digestive tract. This chapter will focus on the problem of reflux and colicky symptoms, which can be very distressing for the entire family. If your baby is persistently fussy, unhappy, and uncomfortable, the likely cause is in the digestive system. Fortunately, there are very effective means of resolving these symptoms with a holistic approach. This chapter will show you the way to solve these very troublesome digestive upsets.

---

breastfeeding

A newborn's job is pretty simple—breathe and eat. Breathing usually happens spontaneously, instinctually, and in a regular pattern, thanks to the nervous system. Eating, however, is a different matter altogether. Once your baby accomplishes the feat of being born, learning to breathe, viewing the world for the first time, and settling down again to sleep, she is pretty much home free. Except that now she needs to eat. What a bother. Fortunately, the breast feels warm and soft, sucking turns out to be very comforting, and mother's milk tastes delicious. Problem solved. Except when mechanical problems interfere with nature's ideal system— the nursing relationship.

Mothers and their babies are attuned to each other. It may take a while to get accustomed to your new baby, and your own feelings may seem overwhelming. The new responsibility, the rush of new hormones, and the depletion that accompanies pregnancy, labor, and birthing can all be a little unsettling. In spite of the difficulties in the first few weeks, new mothers do remarkably well. The budding relationship with your baby blossoms and flourishes. Babies learn from their mothers. They learn how to breathe from being held close to their mother's (and father's) body. They learn how to nurse by the simple physical instructions that are primal and instinctual, communicated by mothers to their babies through love, gentleness, and the natural curves of bodies in harmony. Sometimes a little encouragement by a lactation consultant, midwife, or doctor may facilitate this transition to nursing and smooth any insecurities or rough spots along the way.

Mechanical problems include things like inverted nipples that poke in instead of out, making it difficult for a baby to get milk, inadequate latching on, especially in the "lazy" nurser who dawdles at the breast, and moms who have a vigorous letdown reflex (the signal that sends the milk into the nipple area) that floods the baby too quickly. Some psychological or habitual problems can also occur, things like babies with nipple confusion if they have been offered a bottle or a pacifier at too early an age or babies who are easily distracted by stimuli in the environment and pull off the breast. A lactation consultant should be able to diagnose and help solve these simple nursing problems.

Sometimes immediately and sometimes a little later, infants get into a self-established routine of nursing every couple of hours and sleeping most of the time. Some babies may go for longer periods of time between nursing, and some will want to nurse more often. It's best to allow babies to call the shots and develop their own schedule. Of course, babies come prepackaged with their own personalities. Some are aggressive, voracious feeders. Others are calmer and more sedate, sometimes requiring a little encouragement to stay at the breast. And some babies may never want to leave the breast, even while they're sleeping. Parents need to adjust to the personality and behavioral style of their new baby, and it may take some time to understand the baby's temperament. An active, energetic mom may need to alter her own style of behavior with a quiet and easily disturbed baby. And a mom who normally functions best in a peaceful, calm atmosphere will find it a challenge if she has a spirited, very vocal baby.

The important thing is that babies are gaining weight over the first month of life. Your baby can lose up to 10 percent of her birth weight while the nursing relationship is established and your milk comes in, but by two weeks she should be back to her birth weight and gaining. Most babies gain about six to eight ounces a week, or two pounds per month. Inadequate weight gain usually means some kind of feeding problem exists, which might not even be apparent to you. Or you may know only too well when your baby has digestive or feeding problems. A baby with inadequate weight gain is usually not getting enough milk. This can be due to one of three problems, or a combination:

- **Supply.** Some mothers may have a harder time building up their milk supply. If this is the problem, your baby will seem hungry after nursing. Most infants fall asleep while nursing, or soon after, as if they have been drugged. Older babies may go through growth spurts with greater caloric requirements. They will nurse more to build up the milk supply. A lactation consultant can help with milk supply problems.

- **Temperament.** Some babies may not nurse adequately. These are the distracted or quiet babies who need a little encouragement to stay on the breast. Again, seeing a lactation consultant can be very helpful for these infants.

- **Digestive issues.** Digestive problems may prevent some babies from moving enough milk through their digestive tract. They may spit up excessively, ejecting much of the milk they've drunk, or they may have abdominal cramping that provides negative reinforcement for nursing. The remainder of this chapter will address these issues.

Of course, babies who do not gain weight may have an underlying disease or structural problem that should be investigated by a pediatrician. And sometimes babies have difficulties with nursing or there are health problems that may require the introduction of formula under the direction of a pediatrician and lactation consultant.

identifying digestive problems

Most babies start out just fine—eating, sleeping, looking around at the lights and colors in the new world around them. Most continue on that way. But some have a harder time, getting fussy, crying for no apparent reason, and generally looking uncomfortable, sometimes for hours at a time. Parents worry about their baby's discomfort, and they attempt measures to relieve it. Since parents usually attribute these behaviors to gas, they will search for solutions to these gassy symptoms. Doctors in the past labeled these symptoms as "colic." Today they are attributed to reflux, short for gastroesophageal reflux, sometimes called GERD (gastroesophageal reflux disease) if the symptoms are more pronounced (Vartabedian 2007). Whatever the term, these babies need relief of their troublesome symptoms, and holistic medicine can provide effective treatment without side effects.

Is This a Disease?

Calling a set of symptoms a disease serves two purposes. It may give us some reassuring terms that place the symptoms in a defined context. If parents have babies with colic or reflux, then they can talk about their experiences with others, do Internet research, form support groups, and read books about these conditions in their search for helpful suggestions. The second motivation to call these sets of symptoms a disease is to enable prescription medical treatment for the condition. Conventional medicine had no treatment for colic, but reflux can be treated with drugs. Pediatricians have welcomed the understanding of reflux because they can write a prescription for it. Babies normally spit up. If their symptoms tend to be more severe, the stomach acid coming up irritates the esophagus. Drugs are available to reduce or stop the production of stomach acid. Babies who spit up after eating, arch their backs, cry and scream a lot, and are difficult to console are diagnosed with GERD, and they usually get a pharmaceutical prescription. But studies have not shown that the symptoms of fussy babies are relieved by these prescription drugs (Orenstein et al. 2009).

Chinese medicine has observed these symptoms for three thousand years and attributed them to certain energetic patterns in babies, using other types of terminology (food stagnation, Stomach Qi rising, Spleen Dampness, and Spleen deficiency). Whatever we call these symptoms, they can be very difficult for parents and frustrating for doctors.

Since the 1950s, colic was diagnosed by the symptoms involved, the most prominent of which included excessive crying and difficulty consoling babies by rocking or jostling. Since video recordings found that most babies cried an average of two hours per day, the diagnosis of colic was established as crying for *more* than two hours per day. Mothers tended to attribute these symptoms to gas and abdominal discomfort, but abdominal X-rays of colicky babies discovered no differences in the amount of intestinal gas in babies who cried a lot and babies who did not. Others claimed that an immature digestive tract was responsible for the digestive upset, but biopsies of the intestinal linings of these babies again showed no typical abnormalities or immaturity. Causes and effective treatment remained a mystery.

Then along came the diagnosis of reflux, replacing the outdated idea of colic. This diagnosis was again determined on the basis of symptoms: inconsolable crying, arching the back to escape from the pain, frequent spitting up, sleep disturbance, and poor weight gain. These were essentially the same symptoms that had previously led to the term "colic." Gastroenterologists theorized that excess acid backing up from the stomach led to inflammation of the esophagus and subsequent discomfort. A certain amount of spitting up is normal in babies. In other words, *all* babies have reflux. The diagnosis of disease is based on the theoretical *amount* of reflux. When enough symptoms present themselves, the diagnosis becomes GERD. Presently, 20 to 30 percent of babies are diagnosed with reflux—about the same number who were previously diagnosed with colic (Nelson 1997). But now these babies are prescribed acid-blocking drugs with significant side effects, drugs that have not been proven safe or effective in relieving the symptoms. Some pediatricians now belittle the less invasive treatments that had been recommended for the treatment of colic—swaddling, increased carrying and holding, rocking, and diet changes (Vartabedian 2007). Now a drug prescription is given to help improve the symptoms involved. If that drug doesn't work, then two or more of the currently popular drugs are used together. These drugs are usually acid blockers and antacids. Sometimes these prescriptions initially improve symptoms, but this effect tends to wear off, and babies then return to their previous uncomfortable state. And the drugs themselves may cause significant health problems.

A more effective strategy requires a holistic approach that treats the underlying reasons for the symptoms while instituting measures that relieve symptoms.

What About Lab Tests?

Reflux is almost always diagnosed on the basis of parents' reports of symptoms. However, lab tests may be used for diagnosis in cases where symptoms persist despite interventions and for babies with significant vomiting who may have an obstruction of the digestive tract. The conventional lab tests for reflux are all invasive.

Typical lab tests include a pH probe that sits in the esophagus. The probe transmits readings of acidity through a nasal tube to a recording device outside the baby's body, gathering data over a twenty-four-hour period. The problem with this strategy is that all babies have some degree of reflux of stomach acid into the esophagus (because they all spit up to some degree), and this test may not even prove that the reflux is causing symptoms.

The other commonly used tests are an *endoscopy*, where a scope is used to visualize the esophagus and stomach with the baby under sedation, and an upper GI X-ray of the stomach and esophagus. Endoscopy is usually reserved for severe cases where damage to the esophagus is suspected. And X-rays help determine structural abnormalities, such as blockages in the digestive tract that prevent food from passing freely through the esophagus, stomach, or small intestine. Since symptoms of fussy babies do not seem to correlate well with lab tests, their usefulness is limited. However, if symptoms are severe and persistent or structural problems are suspected, then tests like these can be invaluable in diagnosing serious problems.

Allergy testing that can detect food sensitivities may also be indicated. I will discuss appropriate tests and the holistic perspective of treatment in the following sections, a perspective that provides solutions for beleaguered parents of these uncomfortable babies.

---

symptoms of digestive problems

New babies spend a great deal of energy digesting milk in the first few months. Because eating and digestion are your baby's primary activities in these early days, this is the area where troublesome symptoms happen. A baby's health problems can often be attributed to issues of digestion, even when the symptoms occur in other parts of the body. For example, skin eruptions may have their cause in faulty digestive function, and chronic respiratory congestion can frequently be traced to digestive imbalances. All of these problems will be addressed in detail in subsequent chapters. Parents with fussy babies naturally look to the digestive tract when attempting to solve the problem, and justifiably so.

Crying

Babies cry for a variety of reasons. Crying is a reaction to discomfort, it communicates a problem, and it gets quick attention: "I'm hungry!" "Check my diaper. It's wet." "I'm cold!" "I'm hot." "I hate my car seat." "I'm in pain." And the origin of discomfort in babies is most often their digestive tracts.

Chinese medical texts refer to digestive symptoms, colic, and reflux as night crying. *Heart Methods of Patterns and Treatment in Pediatrics*, an important text in Chinese traditional medicine, explains the notion this way:

> This disease mainly appears in newborns. During the day they are normal, but as they enter the night there is crying and restlessness. Each evening at the same time there is crying. If severe, this may continue throughout the night until dawn. Thus, it is called night-crying. (Flaws 2006, 76)

As this text makes clear, babies tend to be fussy in the evening and at night. Lying down may worsen discomfort if there is a significant reflux component. As I've mentioned, almost all babies have some degree of reflux. The *cardiac sphincter* (the constricting ring that closes off the esophagus where it enters the stomach) is not fully developed in infants. Therefore, some degree of spitting up is normal. When it is excessive, stomach acid will irritate the esophagus and throat. Gravity often helps these babies by keeping stomach acids and milk in the stomach rather than the esophagus. In Chinese medicine, the Stomach/Spleen energetic system is responsible for digestion. When Spleen Qi is weak or deficient, then Stomach energy tends to move up instead of down, resulting in more spitting up, acid reflux, and stagnation of food in the stomach, which contributes to discomfort and crying. Holding your baby upright is likely to improve these symptoms, but strengthening the digestive system will result in more permanent and profound relief of the cause of these symptoms. Stomach energy will start moving down and flow in the right direction. Food will leave the stomach with the proper movement and flow, relieving the stagnation that causes pain.

Besides crying, the typical uncomfortable baby may have other symptoms as well. Your baby may spit up or vomit, tense up her abdominal muscles and pull up her legs, arch her back to escape the pain, and sometimes have loose or watery stools. If stomach acid is irritating the throat, then babies may have persistent coughing. Some parents also notice that babies will make unusual swallowing motions. Babies may be so uncomfortable that their appetite is impaired and they don't want to eat. Pediatricians become concerned when these babies are not gaining weight adequately. Most babies gain six to eight ounces per week, or two pounds per month in the first three months of life. Gaining less than this usually indicates inadequate intake of milk, too much spitting up, or poor absorption of nutrients.

Why do these symptoms typically begin at a few weeks of age? No one really knows why babies are fine for a few weeks and then begin developing symptoms. One hypothesis is that allergy or food sensitivity takes time to develop. Babies' immune systems require time before they begin responding to allergens. It takes extended exposure to irritating or allergenic proteins before babies react with symptoms. Proteins from foods that the breastfeeding mother has eaten are passed through the breast milk, ingested by the baby, and then irritate the lining of the small intestine, damaging the cells that provide a protective barrier against foreign proteins. If the intestinal lining is damaged, then protein molecules make their way into the bloodstream, where they can provoke antibody formation and an allergic response or inflammation in the digestive tract or in other tissues in the body.

A second hypothesis for the onset of symptoms at around three weeks of age is that babies who have problems with digestion may require a few weeks of feeding before the amount of milk consumed is large enough to cause bothersome irritation and symptoms of spitting up and pain.

the problem with drugs

Conventional medical treatment for reflux typically includes drugs that inhibit gastric-acid production. The theory is that if stomach-acid production is blocked, then acid will not irritate the stomach and esophagus. However, stomach acid is there for a reason—to help in digestion and to inhibit harmful bacteria. The drugs used to treat reflux fall into two categories: H2 blockers such as ranitidine (Zantac) or famotidine (Pepcid), and proton pump inhibitors such as omeprazole (Prilosec) or lansoprazole (Prevacid). Histamine 2 (H2) is a chemical that triggers the release of stomach acid. Blocking its action reduces the signal for acid production. Proton pump inhibitors block the enzyme that triggers the last step in stomach-acid production. They are much more potent drugs than H2 blockers.

Unfortunately, these drugs do not address the underlying problems of reflux (an impaired digestive tract), and they may cause other illnesses and digestive problems. Infants prescribed gastric-acid inhibitors of either category have an increased risk of pneumonia and digestive-system infections than healthy children, even after treatment is discontinued. A study of children aged four to thirty-six months treated by gastroenterologists revealed that those children treated with Zantac or Prilosec had an increased risk of pneumonia and gastroenteritis during treatment and in the four-month period following drug treatment (Canani et al. 2006). The incidence of these diseases was attributed to the inhibition of white blood cell function as a direct result of these drugs and to the change in gastrointestinal microflora (the "good" bacteria that assist in digestion) induced by the drugs. For example, children given gastric-acid inhibitors have an increased number of beta-hemolytic strep, the bacteria that cause pneumonia.

Drugs in the proton pump inhibitor category, such as lanso-prazole, have been shown to be ineffective and to cause similar side effects. In one study, there was no difference in symptoms attributed to reflux in infants as a result of taking Prevacid compared to placebo, but the treatment group had a significantly higher incidence of respiratory-tract infections (Orenstein et al. 2009). In a systematic review of all studies evaluating the effect of proton pump inhibitor drugs on reflux, the authors concluded that studies show no effectiveness of these drugs compared to placebo (Karkos and Wilson 2006).

Simethicone (Mylicon) is a drug used to break up gas bubbles in the intestine and is often recommended for gassy, crying babies. Several studies have shown no effectiveness of simethicone in the treatment of colicky symptoms in infants compared to placebo (Metcalf et al. 1994).

the four-step holistic treatment plan

Since drugs are not the answer to reflux and crying babies, another method for treating these symptoms is necessary. Fortunately, a holistic treatment plan will provide relief for these babies and usually completely resolve their symptoms. If your baby does a lot of screaming, seems uncomfortable, is spitting up and having pain, or has a lot of gas with discomfort, then following a four-step management plan will start your journey to alleviating your baby's symptoms. I've listed the steps, and we'll explore each in detail:

1. **Solve feeding issues.** The first step is to address any feeding problems that may contribute to your baby's discomfort. This includes breastfeeding problems and other physical issues.

2. **Stay close.** Try comforting your baby with constant holding and carrying, perhaps aided by using a sling.

3. **Address food sensitivities.** Your baby may be sensitive to foods that she's eating. Breastfed babies are often sensitive to the foods that their moms have eaten. Eliminating those foods may ease a lot of symptoms.

4. **Get professional assistance.** Seek holistic pediatric care and treatment with herbs and other nutritional supplements. Chiropractic care and acupuncture can

also be helpful in establishing balance in your baby's system and relieving discomfort.

Address Any Feeding Problems

Breastfeeding usually goes smoothly once moms and babies get the idea and establish a routine for nursing. However, there are several breastfeeding problems that can lead to symptoms in your baby. The first step in evaluating a persistently crying baby is to make sure that you and your baby have a well-established feeding technique. That means your baby is latching on to the nipple well and nursing without too much gasping and air swallowing, and that you're getting your baby to burp after nursing on each breast. A common problem for babies is an overabundant or overactive milk supply with a forceful letdown reflex. This can overwhelm babies, making them gasp in their efforts to keep up with the flow of milk, resulting in a lot of swallowed air. Changing nursing positions, taking brief breaks in the nursing session, and frequent burping can all help in this situation. If you suspect that nursing is not going well or if you are not confident about your breastfeeding technique and the harmony of the nursing relationship, then seek help. Contact a lactation consultant and your local La Leche League representative.

Swallowing air is a significant cause of distress in babies, and some babies have a tendency to swallow more air than others when they nurse. This problem is compounded if your baby has trouble burping. Frequent burping is usually a good thing. It will prevent the symptoms caused by swallowed air and will help to keep a lazy nurser awake throughout the feeding. Here are some simple techniques to induce a burp:

■ Hold your baby against your chest with her head on your shoulder and gently tap her back.

- Sit her upright on your lap with one hand against her chest and supporting her chin while patting her back with the other hand.

- Lay your baby across your knees with her head higher than her chest.

A cloth diaper or towel will catch any wet burps. For fussy babies, burp every five minutes while nursing or after every ounce during bottle feeding. Keep your baby in an upright position after nursing for at least fifteen minutes, or even longer if she has a tendency to spit up easily. If your baby cries and wakes during sleep, try gently burping her then as well. She may go back to sleep.

Some doctors suggest feeding solids to small babies as a way to create more weight in the stomach to keep food from backing up into the esophagus. I strongly recommend you avoid giving solids to your baby until at least five months of age and avoid cereal and all grains until twelve months. Infants are not equipped to handle solid foods like cereal. They do not yet have the digestive enzymes to break down complex carbohydrates, and the protein molecules in grains can trigger allergic reactions. Some studies show a relationship between eczema and the early introduction of solids. One study found that infants who received solids at eight to twelve weeks of age had a higher incidence of eczema by age twenty-four months (Forsyth et al. 1993). Another study found that preterm infants who were fed solids before seventeen weeks post-term had a significantly higher risk of eczema by age twelve months post-term (Morgan et al. 2004). Do not start introducing potentially irritating foods that may very well worsen your baby's symptoms. There are much better and more efficacious approaches to your baby's crying and digestive disturbance.

Doctors may also be quick to suggest changing from breast milk to formula or supplementing breast milk with formula if your baby is not gaining enough weight. You may start questioning the quality of your milk and the adequacy of your milk supply since your baby is crying and upset after eating. Breast milk is by far the best source of nutrition for your baby. Supplementing with formula tends to cause nipple confusion. Babies who receive bottles may start refusing to breastfeed because the bottle releases milk with much less sucking effort. And formula may aggravate the problem, causing further irritation of the digestive tract. Seeking holistic care will ease your baby's symptoms, and there are also excellent ways to increase milk supply that a lactation consultant or La Leche League leader can suggest. Your holistic medical provider can also prescribe herbs and supplements to address slow milk production. For example, fenugreek (two to four capsules, three times per day) is often effective alone or in combination with other herbs to increase your milk supply within a few days.

Stay Close to Comfort Your Baby

A fussy, easily irritated baby is often comforted by attention, holding, and motion. Some babies respond remarkably well to this kind of attention. But other babies, especially those with physical causes of discomfort like reflux, do not respond well at all and may be irritated by too much jostling. That may be why the studies that examine the effect of holding and carrying on fussy babies are inconsistent. Some studies show that increasing the amount of time that babies are held improves crying and fussiness (Hunziker and Barr 1986), while other studies show no effect on colic from increased holding (Lucassen et al. 1998). This variability may also be a function of different temperament types. While some babies like distraction and activity, other babies prefer quiet and a low level of stimulation. You will need to experiment and discover the techniques that work best for your baby's temperament.

Comforting your baby is accomplished primarily by holding and providing motion. Your baby has been rocked by your body's motion for nine months. A newborn baby is not fully developed and still needs that secure environment of being held and bundled. She will feel soothed by the same fluid sensation of being in your arms or a baby sling while you walk or by being gently bounced at your shoulder. Putting gentle pressure on a baby's abdomen will often help relieve tension there. You can do this by holding your baby facedown with her body stretched along the length of your arm. Or fold your baby's legs against her tummy while she's in your arms, either facing toward you or facing outward.

Swaddling your baby in a receiving blanket during the first few months is an excellent way to make her feel secure. Newborns like to be wrapped tightly in your arms or in a blanket. Swaddling has proven effective in reducing the amount of excessive crying in babies (Van Sleuwen et al. 2006). When babies are wrapped in a blanket they tend to wake less often, and swaddling increases the amount of REM (rapid eye movement) sleep (Gerard, Harris, and Thach 2002). Bundled babies sleep better and cry less. Wrap your baby with her arms across her chest, not down at her sides. She will be most comfy in the fetal position, with her legs also pulled up against her abdomen. Gentle motion often helps fussy babies as well. Wear your baby in a sling. Give her a warm bath. Turn on some comforting music. Try different approaches at different ages, and you will find the one that works best for her.

Reflux symptoms are helped by gravity, which will tend to keep stomach contents where they belong. Holding your baby in an upright position (especially for twenty minutes after eating) will help. A front carrier can be helpful. Laying your baby on her left side will help keep stomach contents away from the esophagus. Laying your baby on her belly while you hold her in your arms or across your lap will usually alleviate symptoms, while a tummy-up position tends to aggravate symptoms. However, mattresses exude a toxic gas, and it's important to keep your baby's nose and mouth away from those fumes while she's lying on a mattress and not have your baby lying facedown unattended for any extended period of time. To avoid the issue of mattress fumes altogether, you can purchase an organic mattress or cover the mattress with polyethylene sheeting to prevent those toxic fumes from causing respiratory problems in your baby. Instructions for mattress covering can be found in my book *Child Health Guide* and on my website at www.cure-guide.com.

A screaming baby upsets everyone. Parents don't want to hear their baby crying in distress. If simple techniques of handling and feeding adjustments are not successful, then other physical causes of crying need to be investigated and further holistic medical interventions are warranted.

Address Food Sensitivities

Your baby's digestive tract is very sensitive. The lining of the small intestine is easily irritated by substances that a baby ingests. That's why it's important to investigate if your baby's distress may be caused by allergens in her food.

Breastfed Babies

Chemicals and proteins that a mom eats will find their way into her breast milk, and these can serve as irritants to a baby's digestive mechanisms. Exposure to these protein molecules can also lead to allergic responses in babies who are sensitive to them because of a genetic predisposition to allergies or because of previous damage to the immune system caused by drugs. The two most common drugs that impair immune function in babies are antibiotics and vaccines. Antibiotics destroy healthy intestinal bacteria that are essential for proper digestion and absorption of nutrients. Vaccines may tend to switch babies' immune systems to a reactive mode that makes them more prone to allergic responses to foods.

If your baby is crying and upset, one of the first things you can do is eliminate chemicals from your diet that might be aggravating her symptoms. According to one study, the chemicals most likely to contribute to crying are caffeine, alcohol, and food additives. Many mothers find that when they eat certain foods, their babies will soon after begin to be upset and have a bad day. These moms quickly learn to avoid those foods. At other times, the aggravating foods might not be so obvious. In that case, remove the most common irritating foods and observe your baby's response when you add them back into your diet one at a time. The most common of these foods are dairy products, chocolate, spices, beans, and vegetables in the cabbage family. Other possible culprits are peanuts, eggs, and wheat. So many babies are sensitive or allergic to dairy that this is the best food to eliminate first. Often just eliminating milk and other dairy products will resolve discomfort in babies, and many mothers find that as soon as they eat any dairy products their babies get worse. Other babies do not react at all to milk or any other allergens.

Studies also confirm that eliminating common allergenic foods from breastfeeding mothers' diets reduces the amount of crying in colicky babies. The foods eliminated in one study included cow's milk, eggs, peanuts, tree nuts, wheat, soy, and fish (Hill et al. 2005). However, the infants in this study only improved by an average of a 21 percent reduction in crying after one week on the elimination diet, and the mothers' assessment of crying did not differ between the treatment and control groups. This suggests that for the majority of infants other interventions will also be necessary.

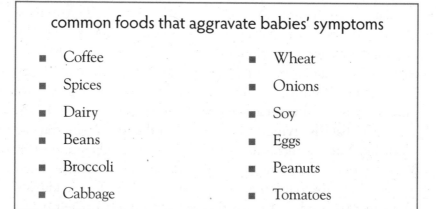

common foods that aggravate babies' symptoms

- Coffee
- Spices
- Dairy
- Beans
- Broccoli
- Cabbage

- Wheat
- Onions
- Soy
- Eggs
- Peanuts
- Tomatoes

Formula-Fed Babies

Babies who are fed formula are especially susceptible to allergies. The most common reasons that a baby needs formula include adoption or a mother who must take medications that would be harmful to her baby if she breastfed. Occasionally a breastfeeding mother cannot provide adequate milk to her baby, and a supplemental formula may be needed. Or mothers may need to get back to work and will supplement their breastfeeding with formula.

Organic formulas are readily available. These formulas do not contain pesticides, hormones, or antibiotics. Be sure to use an organic formula that uses lactose as the added sugar and not sucrose or corn syrup. However, even organic formulas contain cow's milk proteins that can irritate the intestinal lining of babies and stimulate allergic responses. Some other formulas use predigested cow's-milk protein to avoid allergic reactions (Alimentum, Nutramigen, and Pregestimil). These hypoallergenic formulas prevent the irritation that whole milk proteins cause in sensitive babies. However, these formulas are not organic and are highly processed. Your holistic pediatric specialist should be able to advise you about the best sources for your baby if she must have formula.

Soy-milk formulas are not appropriate for babies. They contribute to a wide range of problems, including impaired thyroid function and impaired calcium metabolism. For a thorough discussion of the health problems associated with ingestion of soy products, see the book *The Whole Soy Story*, by Kaayla Daniel (2005). Several countries around the world have forbidden the use of soy formula because of the health risks involved in its use. A large percentage of babies who are allergic to cow's milk will also develop an allergy to soy protein. Other forms of alternative formulas made from rice or nuts do not provide adequate nutrition for small babies either. Breastfeeding is always best because breast milk provides the most suitable food for your baby and the best protection from infections and the development of allergies.

Babies on formula need to have additional supplements. The most important of these is bovine colostrum, which can help to replace the immune-enhancing effect of breast milk. Colostrum, the milk produced in the first few days following birth, contains a host of immune activating and antibacterial constituents. In addition, all babies need omega-3 fats for brain development and adequate immune function. Supplementing formula with fish oil will supply these important fats. Flax oil is not a suitable alternative because babies usually don't produce enough of the enzyme that converts the omega-3 fat in flax (alpha-linolenic acid or ALA) to docosahexaenoic acid (DHA), the fat necessary for the developing nervous system.

---

treating digestive symptoms

The holistic treatment of reflux and digestive disturbances may involve one or more interventions. These can be put in place one at a time, in succession, or more than one can be started simultaneously. The most effective methods, discussed here, include probiotics, herbal treatment, acupuncture, chiropractic care, and homeopathy.

Establish a Healthy Gut Environment

Since reflux and other digestive symptoms such as gas and diarrhea manifest in the gut of sensitive babies, the first step in treatment is to create the healthiest digestive tract possible. Digestion requires adequate intestinal bacteria colonies that gradually develop in the newborn and infant. Your newborn has no intestinal bacteria prior to birth. After exposure to the birth canal, the mother's skin, and breast milk, the gut is colonized with the normal flora necessary for digestion and maintenance of healthy intestinal function. If a healthy gut flora is not established or if babies are treated with antibiotics that destroy these valuable organisms, then digestion of milk will not go smoothly. Since we don't know when and if a baby has developed healthy bacterial colonies, any baby with digestive symptoms should be given live bacteria as a supplement to ensure a healthy gut ecology.

A supplement containing *Lactobacillus* and *Bifidobacterium* species is indicated for distressed babies. Babies who are solely breastfed have colonies of *Bifidobacterium* species, but these bacteria may be deficient due to antibiotics given to mothers or babies or for other reasons. Special supplemental formulas of these bacteria are made for the breastfeeding baby to take on a daily basis. A study of crying (colicky) infants showed that 95 percent responded positively to a probiotic supplement containing *Lactobacillus reuteri*. The assumption of the study's authors was that colic may be associated with an allergic component that would respond to this bacterium, since *L. reuteri* has been successful in the treatment of allergies (Savino et al. 2007). This study would suggest that *Lactobacillus* species including *L. reuteri* can be beneficial to solely breastfed crying babies in addition to *Bifidobacterium* strains. Of course, formula-fed infants will similarly benefit from this supplementation. These supplements are all available in a powder form that can be dissolved in milk. See appendix 1, on medications and supplements, for specific sources.

Professional Assistance to Relieve Symptoms

The mainstays for relief of these digestive symptoms in holistic pediatrics are herbal formulas and homeopathic medicines. Chinese medicine interprets reflux and colic as food stagnation and a weakness of the Stomach/Spleen energetic systems, which are responsible for digestion and assimilation of nutrients. The energy of the Stomach moves down. When a weakness or disturbance occurs, then Stomach Qi will move up, producing reflux and vomiting. The Spleen energy system is responsible for digestion and the movement of fluids in the body. The Spleen also generates Nutritive Qi, which nourishes and provides the energetic foundation for other body systems, including the body's defenses (Wei Qi) and immune function.

Chinese medicine provides tools for directly strengthening the digestive system (the Stomach/Spleen network) using herbs and acupuncture. The primary herbal formula for digestive disturbance in babies is Grow and Thrive (produced by Chinese Medicine Works), a nutritive tonic that promotes the assimilation of nutrients and the movement of food through the intestines. This formula was designed to strengthen and support proper digestive function. It is based on the classical formula Kang Ning Wan, or Curing Pill. Its primary ingredients, hyacinth bean, Chinese yam, lycium, and poria, support the Stomach/Spleen network and build Qi. A secondary herbal formula for reflux and colicky symptoms is Tummy Tamer (Chinese Medicine Works). This formula regulates the function of the digestive system, activating and dispersing the stomach and intestines to move food smoothly along. This formula is based on the fourteenth-century prescription Bao He Wan (Pill for Indigestion). Its primary ingredients, hawthorn, tangerine, radish, bitter orange, and fennel, aid digestion by activating the stomach and small intestine while dispersing and descending the Stomach Qi. Since discomfort and distress in infants is often due to stagnation of food and insufficient movement of food through the digestive tract, a dispersing formula will help to move things along. Other ingredients dispel the accumulation of toxins from food stuck in the stomach and intestines. These prescriptions are available through any licensed health care provider (either one trained in Chinese medicine or a conventional MD), and you should be sure to consult a professional for prescriptions and dosage information.

■ Case Report ■
Digestive Problems Solved

A five-month-old boy had been born by C-section two weeks early and weighed five pounds at birth. He was given antibiotics in the hospital. He was solely breastfed and was gaining weight, but at six weeks old he began vomiting and would also often spit up after nursing. At this same time, he began coughing every day, a common symptom of reflux. He slept well, eleven to twelve hours at night, and he had no apparent discomfort.

His mom gave him a probiotic supplement at the onset of his symptoms. She eats a primarily vegetarian diet with the addition of dairy, eggs, and some fish. However, she did stop dairy when his symptoms began. She was also giving him a DHA supplement and vitamin D3.

This was a very straightforward case of reflux, and the only treatment he received was the Chinese herbal formula Grow and Thrive, along with treatment of two acupuncture points, Stomach 36 and Spleen 6, using a non-needle, cold-laser technique.

Within one day he was significantly improved and his day care provider wanted to know what his parents had done. When I saw him one week later, he was not coughing and had much less spitting up. That improvement continued, and he required very little treatment after that.

■ ■

Several Western herbal formulas have also been used for the symptoms of reflux or colic. A popular tea containing chamomile, fennel, vervain, licorice, and balm mint was evaluated in a randomized, controlled clinical study and shown to significantly improve the symptoms associated with colic compared to placebo (Weizman et al. 1993). *Gripe water* is a generic name for several Western herb formulas that contain a combination of fennel, ginger, peppermint, and chamomile. I suggest using caution when purchasing the various gripe water preparations. Many have some form of sugar (sucrose or fructose), baking soda, and parabens or methylparaben. None of these are safe for infants. Parabens in particular have been shown to cause hormonal disruption, and they are potential carcinogens (Oishi 2002). Organic forms of gripe water do not contain these additives. These herbs do aid digestion and help calm fussy babies, but Chinese herbal formulas will also strengthen and build digestive function to provide a curative treatment that tends to prevent recurrences of symptoms.

Acupuncture

Acupuncture is an extremely useful adjunct to other treatment modalities for babies with reflux. Stimulation of acupuncture points can be accomplished with needles or non-needle techniques including finger pressure, cold lasers, magnets, or massage of acupuncture channels. Acupuncture is an excellent tool for moving energy, and that is just what your baby needs. Acupuncture will help move energy down, readjust your baby's energy balance, and strengthen Stomach Qi so that food moves downward. In the traditional understanding of energy systems, acupuncture relieves the stagnation of food and the upward surging energy of stomach contents, and calms the crampy discomfort of irritated intestines. Acupuncture is a unique and indispensable tool for readjusting the flow of food through your baby's digestive tract while you're using herbs to strengthen digestive function.

Typical acupuncture treatment will focus on the Spleen and Stomach channels and may include others, depending on the symptoms involved. The points Stomach 36 and 37 and Spleen 6 are standbys. But many other points on a variety of channels can be utilized depending on the presenting symptoms. Tui na acupressure massage and sho ni shin massage are especially valuable treatment options for infants, and they do not require the use of needles. Your acupuncturist can show you safe and effective methods of acupressure to use at home with your baby.

Chiropractic

A baby with persistent crying, distress, and reflux symptoms should be evaluated for structural problems by a chiropractic or osteopathic physician who specializes in children. There are many possible causes of structural abnormalities that could contribute to reflux symptoms. Typically, birth trauma occurs from pulling on the head and rotating the neck. This can occur because of mothers lying on their backs during birth, mothers given drugs that slow the birth process, or cesarean sections that require pulling on the baby to extract her from the uterus. This brute force results in tension in and torsion (twisting) of the upper spine and neck. However, even babies born without these sorts of interventions can suffer physical stress during the birthing process that results in spinal injury. Spinal misalignment can be caused by birth trauma or an injury that occurs sometime after the birth. These misalignments can also be caused by positioning problems initiated in utero, creating postural deviations, such as a baby persistently holding her head in one direction. Chiropractors often attribute the arching of the back seen in babies with reflux to these spinal-cord stress injuries. Chiropractic adjustments will release this tension. Babies may be tender and resistant to touch and pressure on their necks at first, but after a few treatments they become much more settled and relaxed. Taking tension out of the neck will result in relaxation in the spinal cord and fascia and relief of the nerve irritation that can trigger digestive symptoms and crying (Olafsdottir et al. 2001).

An interrelationship exists between the nervous system and the immune system. Problems in your baby's spine and spinal cord can result in immune-system dysfunction as well as digestive disturbance. Alleviating this spinal stress can allow further healing and the re-establishment of balance in the immune system as well (Ohm 2009). Whatever the cause, having your baby checked and treated with gentle chiropractic adjustments will eliminate spinal structural problems as a possible contributing cause of her crying.

Homeopathy: Do It Yourself or See a Practitioner

Whereas Chinese medicine and chiropractic require professional help, you can utilize homeopathy yourself—though seeing a qualified homeopath can help with more intransigent problems. I've seen homeopathy do wonders for reflux and crying babies. Never forget the magic of the correct homeopathic medicine, which can clear symptoms instantly. Of course, for many children the effect of homeopathy is gradual and gentle, though the curative ability of a homeopathic remedy is often marvelous. The synergistic effect of homeopathy in combination with herbs facilitates the healing process. Where chiropractic corrects structural problems and Chinese medicine corrects the energetic imbalance, homeopathy provides a profound energetic stimulus to healing. When you address the nutritional components of symptom production as well, the overall holistic effect covers all bases and produces a dramatic curative process.

To find the correct homeopathic medicine, compare your baby's symptoms to the cluster of symptoms described for each medicine. Find the description that matches your baby the best, and try using that one. Start with a single dose of the homeopathic medicine in a 12C or 30C strength. If symptoms improve, then wait and observe. If symptoms return, then repeat the dose. For small babies, you can crush the tiny pellets and mix them with water or breast milk. You can consult appendix 1 at the end of this book for more detail about using homeopathic medicines at home. For persistent or prolonged symptoms, it would be best to consult a professional homeopath, who can treat the underlying constitution and root causes of the energetic disturbance that causes colic and reflux.

The homeopathic medicine most often indicated on an acute level is *Colocynth*, especially if your baby seems better when you press on her abdomen. *Jalapa* is a colic medicine for babies who cry all night and sleep during the day. *Lycopodium* is used primarily when gas symptoms are prominent and when the late afternoon and evening (four to eight p.m.) are your baby's worst time of day. *Nux vomica* corresponds to an exceedingly irritable baby who is worse in the mornings.

Following, I'll offer more specifics about each of the homeopathic remedies you may find helpful.

Chamomilla. The pains associated with *Chamomilla* are sharp and severe. Babies scream and flail. They must be carried and rocked in constant motion, but they are not satisfied by anything they demand. Older babies will indicate something they want and then throw it. They are beside themselves. The abdomen may be bloated and the loose stools are greenish.

Colocynth. The characteristic of the pain that indicates *Colocynth* as the correct medicine is amelioration from pressure. Babies will pull up their legs, doubling up in apparently excruciating pain. If you put pressure on their abdomen, holding them across your knees or over a shoulder, they will get some relief. They tense up their bloated abdomens in response to the sharp, cramping pain that often comes in waves. They will strain and cry before bowel movements and feel better after passing a stool.

Dioscorea. This remedy can be considered the opposite of *Colocynth*. Children who need *Dioscorea* are worse when bending forward and feel better when arching the back. They tend to have a lot of gas. Symptoms are worse in the morning and better when stretching out flat. They also like to be held upright.

Jalapa. Babies who need *Jalapa* cry all night with pain and discomfort but are fine during the daytime. Symptoms often include watery, sour-smelling diarrhea.

Lycopodium. The symptoms that correspond to *Lycopodium* are worse during the hours between four and eight p.m. Look for lots of bloating and gas with a tendency to constipation. Any pressure on the abdomen aggravates the pain and discomfort.

Nux vomica. Babies with symptoms indicating *Nux vomica* are irritable and worse after eating, but especially troubled in the morning. They are very sensitive to spices and other irritants in the mother's diet.

---

special issues in older babies

When feeding problems and digestive symptoms persist beyond the first few months, if babies continue to spit up large amounts of milk, throw up solids, or continue to scream with abdominal pain that keeps them up at night, then they may require a different treatment regimen than infants. These children often suffer from a damaged intestinal lining in need of repair.

The first issue to consider is the type of solids that babies are eating. Grains fed at too early an age can cause significant problems. I recommend that you keep all grains, including rice cereal and oatmeal, out of your baby's diet until at least twelve months (and longer if she is having any allergic or digestive symptoms). Wheat is especially difficult for babies to handle, and it should be avoided in any baby with symptoms. Similarly, dairy products can cause allergies and sensitivities and can damage the intestines of babies. Wait until ten to twelve months for any dairy products. Then you can try yogurt and cheese. Wait until eighteen to twenty-four months before giving whole cow's milk unless your baby must have formula. Babies need the fat of whole dairy products and not reduced-fat preparations.

Older babies may benefit from having specific tests to pinpoint the issues that underlie digestive symptoms. A comprehensive stool test that examines digestive-enzyme production, inflammatory markers, intestinal bacteria, and yeast cultures can be informative and lead to appropriate treatment. Babies with an overgrowth of yeast (*Candida albicans*) may benefit from supplements including *Saccharomyces boulardii* (a strain of yeast that helps establish normal intestinal flora) and a medium-chain triglyceride oil supplement that contains caprylic acid, a potent antifungal fatty acid. Many babies need some additional digestive-enzyme support. If inflammation is a problem, then the amino acid glutamine in powder form has a potent regenerative effect on the intestinal lining. Glutamine benefits the growth of rapidly dividing cells, providing the nutrition required for the synthesis of new RNA and DNA so that cells can multiply. This is vital for maintaining a healthy lining within the digestive tract, where cells have a rapid turnover rate. When there is digestive inflammation, there is an increased need for glutamine for cell repair and replacement. Other anti-inflammatory supplements include the herbs boswellia and turmeric (curcumin), the enzyme bromelain (extracted from pineapple), and the flavonoid quercetin, which is found in many fruits and vegetables. It is important for children with digestive inflammation to also take adequate amounts of omega-3 fats for their anti-inflammatory effect (fish oil is the most accessible source of these fats). And older children with digestive problems need a broad-spectrum probiotic that includes a variety of *Lactobacillus* and *Bifidobacterium* species. Other nutritional supplements may be needed for healthy digestive function, including pantothenic acid, zinc, hydrochloric acid, and prebiotics, depending on the judgment of a holistic pediatric practitioner (see chapter 8).

These children may have food allergies and food sensitivities. Depending on the child's symptoms, a range of food-sensitivity tests can be informative, including blood IgE, IgG, and stool IgA antibody studies. Often these children have a sensitivity to wheat products (including the proteins in gluten, primarily gliadin). Other grains contain gluten as well. Cow's milk proteins are also irritating to many children's digestive tracts. For these children, the protein molecules cause damage to the intestinal lining, disturbing the intestinal barrier and allowing potential allergens into the bloodstream. These foreign proteins then stimulate antibody production and allergic reactions in other parts of the body. This is the beginning of the process that leads to allergies in so many children. Approximately 70 percent of immune activity occurs in the intestinal lining (Brandtzaeg 1998). For this reason, healing the gut is essential to maintaining a healthy immune system. For a more thorough discussion of the relationship and treatment of digestive and immune-system imbalances see chapter 8.

■ Case Report ■
Severe Reflux and Failure to Thrive

I began seeing a boy when he was seven months old. At that time, his size was well below the fifth percentile on growth charts. He had a very poor appetite and simply refused to eat. He screamed a good part of the day and experienced obvious discomfort, arching his back and spitting up when he did eat. He held himself very stiffly and had the developmental progress of a much younger baby.

His birth history was complicated by a C-section because of a breech presentation, and he was hospitalized on antibiotics for eight days. He was being fed formula because of his disinterest in nursing. When I first saw him, he was already taking a probiotic supplement as well as two drugs for his reflux symptoms.

His initial treatment plan included the herbal formula Grow and Thrive combined with Tummy Tamer. He also began taking glutamine, homeopathic *Colocynth*, and cod liver oil. And he started getting acupuncture.

Within one week he was happier, more content, and smiling a lot for the first time. Within two weeks he was eating more food and crying and fussing much less. And he started to gain weight (eleven ounces in two weeks).

Over the course of a month he became a happy baby, his crying disappeared, and his appetite continued to improve, though he was still very low on the growth charts. After two months he stopped the Tummy Tamer and began taking a more tonifying formula. He would need the Tummy Tamer periodically, and he seemed to do better when he took it.

At ten months of age we got him a stool test that revealed heavy growth of yeast and showed signs of intestinal inflammation and low levels of digestive enzymes. He was then begun on a broader-spectrum probiotic that included *Saccharomyces boulardii* and a medium-chain triglyceride oil to address the yeast overgrowth, and we started giving him digestive enzymes before meals.

At eleven months he was doing better and eating a broader range of foods. Since then he has progressed well with a variety of physical therapies, as well as other herbal formulas, to address his developmental progress. His digestive problems disappeared.

■ ■

prevention of digestive problems

It's impossible to predict whether your baby will develop digestive problems, but you can begin to treat any symptoms as soon as you notice them. This will help to prevent problems from persisting or worsening. If you feel uncomfortable with any aspects of nursing or if your baby does not seem happy and contented with feeding, then seek professional help from a breastfeeding expert. If you suspect any problems with gas or tummy discomfort, then begin giving your baby a probiotic supplement. Be careful about eating foods known to cause digestive upset in babies, and stay aware of your baby's reactions to foods that you have eaten. And seek professional help from a holistic pediatric practitioner if your baby has any digestive problems that persist. Since the digestive tract is so important for your baby's nourishment and development, treating digestive symptoms at an early stage can prevent a cascade of worsening symptoms and other health problems.

summary

Digestion is the center of being in infants, and so harmony *and* disorder in your baby are likely to have their origins in the digestive tract. When any digestive problems occur in your infant, the first order of business, no matter what your baby's history, is to develop adequate colonies of healthy intestinal bacteria by giving a probiotic supplement. If colicky symptoms and reflux are the prominent symptoms, then eliminate potentially irritating foods from Mom's diet that are transferred during breastfeeding or change your baby's formula. If digestive symptoms persist, then consider Chinese herbal treatment to strengthen digestive function. Palliative remedies in the form of homeopathic medicines and herbs can help to relieve symptoms. And finally, seeking chiropractic and acupuncture care for your baby can restore balance and complete the holistic treatment plan that leads to cure.

CHAPTER 3

- - - - - - - - - - -

skin problems

The eyes may be the windows to the soul, but for babies the skin is the window to the immune system. Babies are born with clear skin, then the fun begins—baby acne, rashes, cradle cap, and eczema. Fortunately, a holistic approach is very effective in addressing these sometimes very troublesome problems.

- -

your sensitive baby

Homeopathic theory understands that the body wants to keep imbalances and disease processes at the most superficial level possible. Babies tend to express their first symptoms of these imbalances or illnesses in the skin because the skin is the most superficial level of the body. If these symptoms are suppressed, as they would be with steroid drugs such as hydrocortisone, then the symptoms will come back or appear at a deeper level, usually in the form of other allergies. This theory was formally expounded and demonstrated by Samuel Hahnemann in his seminal 1833 work, *The Organon of Medicine* (2007).

Babies also run hot and develop inflammations easily. Their immune systems are not fully developed, and they have few mechanisms for preventing inflammatory reactions. Babies' livers are immature and do not metabolize toxic chemicals that irritate the skin. Their skin is delicate and easily irritated, and they quickly develop allergic reactions. In this chapter we'll examine the most common skin problems that develop in babies during their first year, including baby acne, cradle cap, diaper rash, and eczema. We'll be spending the most time on eczema, as it is one of the more troublesome skin problems your baby may express.

baby acne

Just when you thought everything was going well with your beautiful new baby and all the relatives are coming into town for a visit, he starts breaking out in pimples. Around two to three weeks of age, about 20 percent of babies start to break out with red bumps or whiteheads on the face and neck. There are several theories regarding the cause of acne in babies. These pimples may occur because of changes in maternal hormones during late pregnancy or the withdrawal of the natural estrogens in your blood stream after your baby's birth. This temporary imbalance of male and female hormones may stimulate the oil glands in the skin. One study showed a correlation between the mother's level of sebaceous-gland activity (the gland that produces oil in the skin) and her baby's secretion of sebum in these same glands, suggesting a correlation between baby acne and maternal hormones (Henderson, Taylor, and Cunliffe 2000).

Some studies have shown that a majority of infants with acne have a type of yeast growth on their skin, either *Malassezia furfur* (Rapelanoro et al. 1996) or *Malassezia sympodialis* (Bernier et al. 2002). But others have found no association with these forms of yeast and the degree of severity of acne in infants (Ayhan et al. 2007).

Treatment of Acne

Regardless of the causes, baby acne is a harmless condition that will fade away by the time your baby is three to four months old, though it can come and go over this period of time. No specific treatment is needed for these pimples.

Prevention of Acne

Giving your baby a probiotic supplement of *Bifidobacterium* (the predominant beneficial intestinal bacteria in babies) may be helpful for its anti-inflammatory effect, and mothers who take an omega-3 fish oil supplement will transfer these fats to their babies through breast milk with the same effect. Babies who are fed formula should always be supplemented with fish oil (see appendix 1 for dosage information).

----

cradle cap

If your baby has dry flakes or unsightly yellow and oily scales on his scalp, you're dealing with cradle cap. This is a harmless condition otherwise known as *infantile seborrheic dermatitis*. Regardless of its somewhat cute name, cradle cap can be annoying and persistent, even into the toddler years and beyond. The intuitive strategy of continually rubbing the cradle cap off your baby's scalp is not usually effective. And, because it is already oily, the common practice of coating it with oil and trying to rub it off may make it even worse.

Treatment of Cradle Cap

Like other skin conditions in children (see eczema), a problem with conversion of essential fatty acids may have a role in cradle cap. One of these essential fatty acids, linoleic acid, may not be converted to gamma-linolenic acid (GLA) because of an enzyme deficiency. GLA is important for healthy skin function. There is some evidence that suggests a temporary deficiency of this enzyme is associated with cradle cap in infants (Tollesson et al. 1993), so supplementing babies with GLA is an important part of the treatment for cradle cap. GLA is available as a supplement in the form of borage-seed oil or evening primrose oil. Applying borage-seed oil directly to the scalp can also be beneficial (Tollesson and Frithz 1993).

Other external applications may help. In a study of patients with seborrheic dermatitis (the "grown-up" version of cradle cap) an extract of aloe vera applied to the scalp proved effective in relief of symptoms in 62 percent of the treatment group compared to improvement in only 25 percent of the control group, who used a placebo cream (Vardy et al. 1999).

For breastfed babies, moms can try also try eliminating foods from their diet that may have a role in allergic reactions. One study found an improvement in infants' cradle cap when their mothers eliminated allergenic foods (especially milk, wheat, and eggs) from their diets (Eppig 1971).

diaper rashes

Diaper rashes come in two forms: irritation (often from chemicals) and an overgrowth of yeast or bacteria on the skin. Irritation can occur as a result of a wet or soiled diaper left on your baby for too long or from chemical residue from laundering diapers or a chemical contained in disposable diapers. Your baby's skin can be easily chafed just by rubbing or from scooting around in a diaper. Sooner or later you are likely to see a rash on your baby's bottom.

Treatment of Diaper Rash

Diaper rash is annoying, but not dangerous. It is rare for an irritated rash to become infected with bacteria. Irritated skin will usually respond to elimination of irritants, application of soothing creams or ointments, and exposure to air. Avoid topical products that contain preservatives (parabens), perfumes, and other petrochemicals because they are absorbed through your baby's skin into his bloodstream. These petrochemicals could have hormone-disrupting effects (Oishi 2002).

Use products that contain calendula and other soothing herbs and lanolin (like Lansinoh) to calm irritated skin. Using a natural zinc-oxide diaper cream like the products made by Weleda will help to create a barrier for the skin so that urine will not come in contact with the rash. Avoid products with lavender because of its potential to cause estrogenic effects. Lavender is suspected of being a potent plant estrogen source (Henley et al. 2007), and the less estrogen exposure your baby has the better. Estrogen promotes abnormal tissue growth and is therefore a carcinogen.

Prevention of Diaper Rash

The first issue to consider is hygiene. Keep your baby's bottom clean. Rashes can develop from bacteria that proliferate on the skin where there is moisture. Change your baby's diaper as soon as he poops and at least every two hours. Make sure that you wipe away all traces of poop, and if your baby is a girl, especially in the folds of her equipment. Keep the creases of your baby's neck clean as well. The milk that drips down from nursing can leave sugar residues that promote bacterial growth there too.

Leave your baby's diaper off for a period of time each day if possible, and certainly if he has a rash. Exposure to air and to the sun will help heal the skin. Yeast especially likes warm, moist, dark places, and sun exposure will discourage yeast growth. Your baby can be left in the sun for extended periods of time if the sunlight is filtered through window glass, which absorbs most of the UV light. And limiting direct sun exposure to twenty minutes will prevent sunburn.

Some foods may be irritating to your baby's bottom. Think of this possibility when a rash appears around your baby's anus. When introducing a new solid, watch for rashes around your baby's mouth and anus. Eliminate the offender for a couple of months, then try it again. Acidic foods like oranges and tomatoes can be irritating, and it is best to wait until your baby is twelve months old before introducing these. Other raw fruits such as melons and strawberries can produce similar reactions. During the first few months of introducing solids, stick to bananas, carrots, yams, green vegetables, and applesauce. Gradually, you can then introduce more foods in the form of pureed soups. Wait until twelve months for grains and dairy products. And wait until eighteen to twenty-four months for any nuts. For a more detailed discussion of solid food introduction, see my book *Child Heath Guide*.

yeast rashes

Your baby's skin is easily colonized with yeast, and some babies are more prone to yeast diaper rashes than other babies. A rash caused by yeast appears as circumscribed areas of redness that spread, and these areas are often surrounded at their edges by many red dots. A yeast rash can also look like bright red, scalded skin. You can see examples by doing an image search on the Internet for yeast diaper rash. Leaving your baby in a wet diaper or wet swimming suit will encourage yeast, while open air and the sun will discourage it. But once yeast rashes occur, they can be stubborn, and they are usually unresponsive to calendula and other soothing creams. You will need to get more aggressive with these rashes.

Treatment of Yeast Rashes

Treating a yeast rash involves using topical applications that discourage yeast and using internal treatments that create an environment that does not allow yeast to proliferate. For babies, this usually means using a probiotic powder both ingested and mixed with a cream for external applications to the skin. The yeast product *Saccharomyces boulardii* will help fight off candida (an overgrowth of yeast) in the gut. Giving your baby a medium-chain triglyceride (MCT) oil derived from coconuts will also discourage yeast as a result of the caprylic acid in the oil.

Mix the oil in some pureed food or just give it straight on a spoon or medicine dropper. MCT oil is derived from coconut oil, which itself has important health benefits, especially for the immune system. But MCT oil is also specific for controlling yeast.

For external treatment, add a probiotic powder to your diaper cream and apply a Chinese herbal preparation that drains Dampness and clears Heat. An excellent product is Yin-Care solution, available to licensed practitioners through Yao Company at www.yincare.com. These products will help to prevent recurrences of yeast. Over-the-counter antifungal creams may improve the rash, but the symptoms often return unless you address the internal environment that makes your baby susceptible to yeast. In severe cases of yeast rashes, you will want to consult with a holistic pediatric practitioner to help you develop a more intensive treatment plan.

Prevention of Yeast Rashes

If you expose your baby's bottom to the air for a period of time whenever possible, that will help to prevent yeast rashes. Make sure to change your baby's diaper as soon as you can after it is wet or soiled.

---

eczema

Eczema, an allergic skin eruption, goes by several names that all mean the same thing. *Atopic dermatitis*, *contact dermatitis*, and *eczema* are all synonyms for allergic skin reactions that often start in infancy, and most children with eczema will develop symptoms by six months of age. Eczema occurs in the form of dry and red eruptions on the cheeks or in dry patches on the trunk and extremities in infants. In older babies and toddlers, it occurs more often in the flexures of the elbows and knees or other folds of skin (neck, ankles, and wrists). The *flexures* (the places where the joints bend) are a site of friction between two skin surfaces, and they tend to be moist and hot. In Chinese medicine, eczema is characterized as a disease of Heat and Damp. It's often itchy in older babies, and they rub their faces on bedding and on your clothing to get some relief. Often the itching becomes awful, keeping babies awake at night and disturbing everyone's sleep. As eczema worsens, the skin cracks, becomes raw, and even bleeds, and it may ooze a fluid discharge that dries as yellow crusts. Eczema can be mild and rashy or severe and infected. A baby with very rosy cheeks may be in the beginning stages of eczema, a precursor to a worsening of the skin symptoms and other allergies as well.

Whatever the stage or severity, these symptoms need to be treated because they are a sign of an internal immune-system imbalance that may manifest in other ways as well. As the problems worsen, symptoms move from the skin inward to the respiratory mucous membranes and the lungs. Thus eczema may progress to asthma and to hay fever as children get older. This constellation of symptoms in children is known as *atopy* or *atopic disease*, a phrase that refers to the allergic process that causes these different symptoms at different ages.

Why Eczema Skin Eruptions Occur

Some babies develop eczema and others do not, and there are several predisposing and precipitating causes that we can discuss. These factors may increase the risk of babies acquiring eczema, but sometimes we just don't know why an individual baby develops these skin symptoms when his siblings are free of skin problems.

Vaccinations

If your baby has a family history of allergies, eczema, or asthma, then he has a higher risk of developing eczema, since these eruptions are a sign of allergic reactions. The offending allergen may not be easy to identify, and tests for allergens may not be accurate in small babies. Genetic tendencies make babies more susceptible to allergies and eczema, but often some stress to the immune system throws babies into an allergic mode of reacting. Environment and physical stress play a major role, especially when combined with a genetic predisposition.

Unfortunately, most babies are exposed to the primary physical stress that triggers a shift in the immune system toward allergic reactions. This stress is vaccination. The reason that vaccines trigger a shift to an allergic mode of the immune system has to do with the way that vaccines stimulate immune responses. The immune response can be separated into two categories: a cellular part that primarily stimulates white blood cells that defend the body by engulfing and destroying microbes and foreign organisms; and a part that primarily creates antibodies that circulate in bodily fluids to defeat foreign invaders. These two types of responses are known as the *Th1 response*, or *cell-mediated immunity*, and the *Th2 response*, or *humoral* (bodily fluid) *immunity*. The two types of responses are in balance, each responding when it is appropriate. Th1 maximizes the killing capabilities of white blood cells that engulf organisms and foreign debris in the body. Th2 responses are characterized by antibody formation in reaction to foreign proteins and include allergic reactions. Vaccines stimulate the Th2 system, forming antibodies to invading microbes. Researchers think that vaccination of children tends to cause a shift in the predominance of Th2 responses and antibody formation, creating an imbalance in immune responses, making children more prone to allergic reactions (Kidd 2003).

This theory has been affirmed by several studies that show a higher incidence of allergies, including eczema and asthma, in vaccinated compared to unvaccinated children. One study showed that vaccinated children were at least twice as likely to develop allergies compared to the unvaccinated (Enriquez et al. 2005). Another study, conducted from data in the National Health and Nutrition Examination Survey on infants through adolescents aged sixteen, showed that children vaccinated with DTP (diphtheria, tetanus, and pertussis) or tetanus alone were twice as likely to develop asthma compared to unvaccinated children (Hurwitz and Morgenstern 2000). A study in Great Britain produced similar findings, associating asthma with the pertussis vaccine. In that study, 243 children received the vaccine and 26 of them later developed asthma (10.7 percent), compared to only 4 of the 203 children who had never received the pertussis vaccine (2 percent). Additionally, of the 91 children who received no vaccines at all, only 1 had asthma. Therefore, researchers concluded that the risk of developing asthma was about 1 percent in children receiving no vaccines and 11 percent for those children who received vaccines, including pertussis (Odent, Culpin, and Kimmel 1994).

Before agreeing to vaccinations for your baby, you should consider the risks involved. Infants in their first year have more reactions to vaccines than older children. For a complete discussion of the risks and benefits of vaccination, see my book *The Vaccine Guide* (Neustaedter 2002).

Allergens

Another stress that can shift babies into allergic reactions is exposure to proteins that trigger antibody responses. Sometimes exposure comes from the foods a breastfeeding mother has eaten. Introducing allergenic solid foods at too young an age can also cause allergic reactions. Some children will be more prone to develop these allergic and hypersensitivity reactions than others, depending on their nutritional status, prenatal environment, and genetics.

Avoiding the early introduction of solids and delaying allergenic foods such as grains, egg whites, and dairy products until babies are at least twelve months old will help to prevent these allergic reactions. If babies already have eczema, then stopping these foods is essential. The early introduction of grains and other solids has been associated with the development of eczema in babies (Forsyth et al. 1993; Morgan et al. 2004). However, other studies have not found that earlier introduction of solids has an effect. Perhaps the conflicting nature of these studies points to another contributing cause for eczema.

The Gut Connection

Besides vaccines, the most frequent contributing cause of eczema is the presence of gut irritation and consequent allergies. A baby with digestive problems is more likely to develop eczema (Rosenfeldt et al. 2004). Irritation of the intestinal lining, typically caused by food molecules contained in breast milk or foods in your baby's diet, may damage the delicate cells that provide an important barrier between the food in the digestive tract and the bloodstream. If large protein molecules leak through a damaged intestinal wall, they can trigger a reaction to these foreign molecules, and antibodies form against them. These antibodies then trigger the inflammatory reactions of eczema (redness, heat, and swelling). Studies have shown a direct correlation between a damaged and defective intestinal barrier and the severity of eczema (Rosenfeldt et al. 2004). As I mentioned earlier, these inflammatory reactions typically occur first in the skin because the body tries to keep them at the most superficial level it can. And the skin is the most visible site where we can observe inflammatory reactions. We can't see the inflammation that may be occurring in the intestinal lining. Eczema is often the first sign of leaky gut syndrome, otherwise known as *impaired intestinal permeability*, in babies. If the offending foods are continued, then damage continues to occur in the intestinal lining and healing does not take place. But once the irritating foods are removed, cells in the intestinal lining are rapidly replaced with new, healthy cells and the protective intestinal barrier is reestablished.

Treatment of Eczema

There are many things you can do to soothe your baby's eczema and help him overcome it once and for all.

Avoid Triggers

The first step in treating eczema is the avoidance of triggers, both allergens and potential irritants. Anything irritating that comes in contact with your baby's skin could aggravate eczema. Be careful about laundry detergents. Even biodegradable products can be irritating to your baby's delicate skin. There are several options. Use a laundry soap that is made from fats treated with an alkali rather than using detergents, which usually have synthetic and harsher ingredients. Try to avoid commercial products with perfumes, which are petrochemicals. An excellent choice is Cal Ben laundry soap (www.calbenpuresoap.com). Another great choice is to use soap nuts. These are actual seeds from a tree that grows in Asia. Add a few in a small cotton bag to your laundry load, and they will clean your clothes without the use of any harsh chemicals. An Internet search should lead you to a supplier of soap nuts, or go to www.maggiespureland.com. Use cotton clothing next to your baby's skin. Synthetic fabrics can be irritating.

If your baby has eczema, then foods that go through your breast milk can trigger reactions. Avoid dairy, eggs, wheat, soy, and corn for starters. Then, after a period of a month, you can reintroduce them one at a time for several days and observe if they cause skin reactions.

Babies who are formula fed cannot avoid dairy, and soy formula is not an appropriate substitute for milk. You can try a hypoallergenic formula such as Nutramigen, Alimentum, or Pregestimil, all of which use predigested cow's-milk protein. These formulas are not the best choice because they are highly processed and sweetened with corn syrup, and they contain soy oil and other vegetable oils along with the more beneficial oils from coconut and palm. They will need to be supplemented with adequate levels of fish oil to supply omega-3 fatty acids. They will, however, prevent allergic reactions to cow's-milk protein.

Be Selective with External Applications

Treating the surface of the body is not an effective plan for eczema because the problem is an internal immune-system issue. Putting things on the skin may be soothing, but it will not address the underlying problems that have caused the skin eruptions. Internal treatment with a holistic approach can be very effective in the management of eczema, but relying on external applications to the skin will ultimately be frustrating. Usually, eczema will eventually go away, often to be replaced by a deeper, more serious allergic disease (such as asthma), especially if the skin eruptions are suppressed with steroid drugs (Hahnemann 2007).

Various types of external applications can be soothing and prevent some of the dryness and skin cracking of eczema, even though they are not curative. Since babies with eczema have dry skin, using moisturizing lotions and oils can be very helpful to prevent the intense dryness and cracking of the skin that can occur. Use only mild and preferably organic bath products and skin lotions on your baby. Avoid any product that contains parabens or lauryl or laureth sulfate. You want to hydrate your baby's skin, but water and bathing are drying to the skin. This is because when you bathe your baby, the hot water will open his skin pores and allow water in, but these open pores will also allow the water to evaporate from the skin when he gets out of the bath. You can prevent this evaporation by covering his skin with oil after a bath. This will seal the water into the skin. You can use olive oil or another mild vegetable oil. You can also use a small amount of essential oil mixed with the vegetable oil, or use a vegetable-based massage oil. Do not use mineral oil or other petroleum-based products. And avoid products that contain lavender, since lavender has estrogenic effects (Henley et al. 2007). Moisturizers will also help keep the skin pliable and prevent drying. Again, use mild and organic products.

Many different lotions are available that can help relieve the itching of eczema. However, these are hit and miss, and you may need to experiment with different products to find one that works for your baby. Some may actually irritate your baby's skin. Those that contain goldenseal, comfrey, calendula, and other herbs work for some parents. Cardiospermum is a plant that can be soothing for eczema. It is commercially available as Florasone Cream, a product of Boericke & Tafel. A chamomile-extract cream applied to the skin was more effective than hydrocortisone in one study (Patzelt-Wenczler and Ponce-Poschl 2000).

Avoid Drugs

The most commonly used drugs for eczema are steroid creams and antihistamine drugs. Steroid creams come in increasingly potent varieties from over-the-counter hydrocortisone to powerful prescription medications. All of these suppress the inflammatory response in the skin, but they are absorbed into the body. The skin is one of the best routes for drug administration. Since steroids work by suppressing the body's immune system, they can have other, unwanted side effects, such as causing skin infections or suppression of the adrenal glands' ability to produce their natural anti-inflammatory steroids. A common side effect is a thinning of the skin where steroids are applied.

Nonsteroidal drugs have also been used as creams to treat eczema; however, two popular eczema drugs have significant side effects. Reports of cancer in patients using these drugs led the FDA to issue a report warning of the link between the popular topical eczema drugs Protopic (tacrolimus) ointment and Elidel (pimecrolimus) cream to a possible increased risk of skin cancer, lymphoma, and respiratory infections in children (U.S. Food and Drug Administration 2005). The FDA received reports of seventy-six cases of cancer among patients using these drugs. This prompted a January 2005 order to place a warning on the drugs stating that their long-term safety has not been established. The report suggested that the drugs not be prescribed for children under two years of age. (The report and warning labels can be found through a search at the FDA website, www.fda.gov, or see the references list.) Both drugs are immunosuppressants—that is, they suppress the body's immune response and inflammation, but they also decrease the body's immune response to cancer and other diseases.

Antihistamines such as Benadryl (diphenhydramine) can provide temporary relief of itching for a few hours, but these antihistamines have side effects. Benadryl is especially sedating and is usually given at night to treat itching. Other antihistamines are not recommended or approved for children under two years of age.

Prevention of Eczema

Stop eczema before it starts. The first key to prevention of skin problems is nutrition. If mom has a healthy diet with an adequate nutrient intake, then baby is less likely to develop skin problems. Eating a whole-foods diet during pregnancy and taking the right nutritional supplements will ensure the best possible outcome from a nutrient perspective. A whole-foods diet consists primarily of foods in their natural state, including fruits, vegetables, and animal products, with a minimal amount of packaged and processed foods. Many studies have shown that babies born to mothers who took a probiotic supplement during pregnancy have less eczema (Lee, Seto, and Bielory 2008; Wickens et al. 2008). The most studied and the most successful probiotic for this purpose during pregnancy is *Lactobacillus rhamnosus* GG. For any baby with a family history of allergies or eczema, mothers can take *L. rhamnosus* during their pregnancy. For several reasons it is advisable for pregnant women to also take a high-potency omega-3 supplement with adequate amounts of eicosapentaenoic acid (EPA) and DHA. This will foster maximum nervous-system development and help to prevent inflammation in mothers and their babies.

A Different Approach to Eczema: Internal Treatment

The effective treatment of eczema usually requires a holistic perspective that includes nutritional supplements and other specific therapies to reduce inflammation and support the immune system. The nutritional supplements we'll be examining are boxed for your easy reference.

---

nutritional supplements for eczema

Fish oil

Gamma-linolenic acid (GLA)

Probiotics (including *L. reuteri* and *L. rhamnosus*)

Vitamin D$_3$ (cholecalciferol)

Colostrum

Since a majority of the immune-system function occurs in the intestines, it is essential that the integrity of the digestive tract be nourished and maintained. A healthy balance of intestinal bacteria and a healthy gut lining are important. And supplementing with a probiotic is always a good idea. Your baby needs the right kinds of fatty acids, and a baby with eczema may have a disorder that calls for additional fat supplementation. Taking a holistic approach to treatment provides relief of inflammation and itching while building a stable immune system that is less reactive. This will make your baby less sensitive to the irritants in the environment or diet that trigger reactions. The goal of internal treatment of eczema is cure—the complete healing of the immune-system disorder that lies at the root of this symptom complex.

Beneficial Fatty Acids

The omega-3 fat EPA in fish oil will help prevent inflammatory reactions. Any child with eczema should be taking a fish-oil supplement. In addition, the omega-6 fatty acid GLA has been proven beneficial for children with eczema. Some studies have shown that the metabolism of essential fatty acids is abnormal in people with eczema, resulting in low levels of GLA. These children are thought to have a deficiency of the enzyme that converts linoleic acid to GLA, resulting in a deficiency of GLA (Horrobin 2000). Supplementation with GLA has proven effective in the treatment of eczema in adults (Andreassi et al. 1997) and in infants (Fiocchi et al. 1994). Supplementing GLA in infants who were at high risk of eczema because of a family history also reduced the severity of later eczema in these children (Van Gool et al. 2003). GLA is available as a supplement derived from borage-seed oil or evening primrose oil. The dosage of GLA in clinical studies ranged from 100 mg to 3 grams of GLA per day.

Healing the Gut

Doing stool tests by a thorough lab such as Genova, Metametrix, or Diagnos-Techs through your baby's health care provider can yield important information about the health of his digestive tract. These tests can detect yeast growth, levels of beneficial and pathogenic bacteria, problems with absorption, and the presence of inflammation, all of which can be treated with holistic methods.

The two strains of beneficial *Lactobacillus* bacteria that seem to have the greatest effect in ameliorating eczema in clinical studies are *L. reuteri* and *L. rhamnosus* GG. Several studies have shown the beneficial effects of these probiotics when given to mothers during pregnancy and to children with eczema. Children treated with *L. reuteri* had a significant reduction of eczema at two years of age (Abrahamsson 2007). In another study, the combination of *L. reuteri* and *L. rhamnosus* resulted in significant improvement in children's eczema when compared to a control group (Rosenfeldt et al. 2003). A follow-up study determined that the improvement of eczema symptoms in those children who used this combination of probiotics was associated with an improvement in the integrity of the intestinal barrier. These children had a decrease in measured permeability of the intestinal lining, which has been associated with leaky gut and the production of antibodies to ingested proteins (Rosenfeldt et al. 2004). The product Primadophilus Reuteri, by Nature's Way, provides both probiotics, *L. reuteri* and *L. rhamnosus*.

Eczema is often complicated by digestive problems, and addressing the digestive component may be an important step in the healing process for your baby. As you will see later in this book, creating a strong immune system means also maintaining a healthy digestive tract.

■ Case Report ■
Reflux and Eczema

I first saw this cute girl (whom I'll call Annie) when she was five months old. Her mom told me that Annie spit up a lot and had awakened every hour during the night for the preceding two months. During the first few months of life she would scream after nursing. When I first saw Annie in my office, she was going for days at a time without a bowel movement, and she seemed uncomfortable. Her mother reported that the delayed stools seemed to make Annie feel uncomfortable, and the baby's sleep was more disrupted as a result. Annie was solely breastfed, except when her mom gave her water if she seemed constipated. Annie's only other symptom was eczema in patches in the flexures of her knees and elbows.

Since the focus of her symptoms was in the realm of digestion, I began treating Annie with probiotics in the form of L. reuteri and L. rhamnosus and a second probiotic with Lactobacillus and Bifidobacterium species. In addition to helping with Annie's digestion, L. reuteri would also address her skin eruptions. I gave her a Chinese herbal mixture containing two formulas, Grow and Thrive combined with Quiet Calm, one dropper twice a day. These two formulas were to address the digestive disorder (Grow and Thrive) and the night waking (Quiet Calm, which has a soothing effect on the shen, or spirit). Both of these are pediatric formulas produced by Chinese Medicine Works (CMW). I asked the mom to eliminate dairy from her own diet.

Two weeks later, Annie's mom reported that Annie was spitting up less and having bowel movements every two days. However, her eczema rashes were still a problem, with red bumps on her arms and persistent eruptions in her flexures.

At that point, we added the herbal formula Fire Fighter to treat the eczema. Annie's mom also began to take a fatty acid supplement with fish oil and borage-seed oil, providing EPA, DHA, and GLA.

One month after she first came in, Annie was sleeping four to five hours at a stretch, she was no longer spitting up, and her skin had dramatically improved.

■　■

Immune System Supplements

Maintaining a healthy immune system depends upon adequate amounts of vitamin D3, either from sun exposure or supplementation. Babies should receive 1,000 IU of vitamin D3 in a supplement during the winter months when exposure to the sun is limited. Toddlers and older children should take 2,000 IU per day.

Another important supplement, especially for babies who aren't breastfed, is colostrum or the beneficial active constituents of colostrum (lactoferrin, alpha-lactalbumin, and immunoglobulins). These are available through fresh cow's colostrum, powdered colostrum, or various supplement preparations. See chapter 8 for a complete discussion of the immune-modulating effects of these supplements. If babies have any sensitivity to cow's milk, then colostrum is not recommended.

Chinese Herbs and Acupuncture

Babies are hot. They are prone to conditions of excess Heat and inflammation, especially if these are triggered by specific stresses that push their systems in this direction. Eczema is an inflammatory reaction and is categorized as a Damp-Heat condition in Chinese medicine. In different children there may be more or less Heat (redness, dryness, itching) or Dampness (secretions, moist skin). And the treatment may vary accordingly. Of course, the picture may be complicated by other factors as well, including digestive-system weakness and respiratory problems, all of which will need to be treated from an inclusive perspective.

Several Chinese herbal formulas have been manufactured specifically for babies to ameliorate these conditions, and I've mentioned them before. The preeminent formulas are produced

by Chinese Medicine Works (available through Kan Herb, www
.kanherb.com). Fire Fighter is a Chinese formula in the Gentle
Warrior pediatric series. It is specifically designed to treat the Heat
and Dampness of childhood eczema and is perfectly safe to use for
babies. The dosage may vary depending on the weight of your
baby and the severity of symptoms. Fire Fighter is a liquid extract
and can be combined with other formulas, depending on your
baby's individual needs. For example, when leaky gut and digestive
disturbances accompany or precede problems with eczema, then
the formula Grow and Thrive may be indicated to strengthen the
digestive and immune-system component of your baby's symptom
picture. If related respiratory problems are also involved, then specific formulas may be needed to treat the Dampness and Phlegm as
well. Other manufacturers also have complementary formulas that
can be utilized to treat specific symptom complexes and imbalances in your individual baby. An acupuncturist with training in
pediatrics will be able to prescribe the correct herbal formula that
will act curatively for your baby.

Acupuncture similarly has the ability to relieve Heat and
Dampness. Typical points used in acupuncture treatment include
the combination of Spleen 10, Large Intestine 11, and Urinary
Bladder 17 to disperse Heat, Stomach 40 to treat Dampness, and
Stomach 36 and Spleen 6 to strengthen digestive function. These
points and others can be stimulated with needles or with noninvasive methods (laser, magnets). Many acupuncturists will also use
different forms of massage of acupuncture points and meridians.
When combined with herbal treatment, these acupuncture techniques will help to relieve the symptoms of itching and inflammation. They will also build the strength of the system and help your
baby's body heal the imbalance.

■ Case Report ■
Severe Eczema Cured

A five-month-old boy I'll call Sam began having eczema eruptions on his cheeks at age three months. The eruptions quickly worsened and spread to his extremities, and the itching would wake him every hour or two in the night. His hands were frequently at his scalp, scratching away. His parents had used hydrocortisone applications and Aquaphor as a moisturizer. He wore only cotton clothing and these were washed in Dreft laundry soap (a gentle formulation for babies). He was solely breastfed, and his mother avoided wheat and eggs. Sam's stools were frequently watery and contained sticky mucus. He was otherwise a happy and easy baby, with no screaming or apparent discomfort except for the itching.

Because of the severity of his symptoms, we put Sam on a pretty rigorous supplement program that included a probiotic formula that also contained *Saccharomyces boulardii* to treat possible yeast overgrowth, borage-seed oil to supply GLA, glutamine powder (one half teaspoon) to support his intestinal function, and cod-liver oil to supply omega-3 fats (one half teaspoon). Mom stopped consuming dairy products. Sam received a Chinese herbal prescription that included the formulas Grow and Thrive, Fire Fighter, and Purge External Wind, the Grow and Thrive (CMW) to support digestive and immune function, the Fire Fighter to treat inflammation and Heat in the skin, and Purge External Wind as additional treatment for the itching. We also began to treat him with acupuncture for both his digestive and inflammation symptoms.

Within a week of initiating treatment Sam's stools improved. They were no longer watery and contained no mucus. He had less scratching and his sleep improved. He continued to have acupuncture once a week on an ongoing basis. His itching would come and go over the next two months, and we changed his herbal prescription to Fire Fighter plus Purge Damp Heat (CMW). This combination addressed the allergic inflammation and his tendency to accumulation of Dampness, indicated by the mucus in his stools and his oily, moist-looking skin. After that, his skin improved significantly. Sam continued to have acupuncture treatment and his skin symptoms gradually faded away.

■ ■

Homeopathy

A constitutional homeopathic medicine prescribed by a qualified homeopath can act miraculously in babies. This may be the one factor that provides an intense boost to healing in your baby. Superficial medicines intended to relieve itching will do little for eczema, since this is an internal problem that requires a deep-acting medicine. Eczema is not a condition for home prescribing. The constitutional medicine is chosen on the basis of the total symptom picture, taking into account genetic predispositions and your baby's temperament, unique characteristics, and physical symptoms.

Parents, however, should be cautious about using a homeopathic medicine as the initial treatment step in eczema. Since eczema presents itself in such a volatile external manner, it's possible for a homeopathic constitutional medicine to cause a significant aggravation of the skin symptoms. Your baby's body is already expressing symptoms through an inflammation on the surface. Homeopathy works by providing a strong stimulus to healing. This may result in an even stronger effort by the body to expel toxins or move an energetic imbalance out of the body through the skin. I start treatment with immune-system support and treatment of the inflammation first, then use a homeopathic medicine to boost the healing process.

Eczema: What to Expect During Treatment

Eczema comes in many forms and degrees. Some babies have red, chapped-looking cheeks. Others get occasional rashes in the flexures of their elbows and knees. And some unfortunate little ones have red, inflamed eruptions that may cover large areas of their bodies with the torment of itching that keeps them (and their parents) awake for much of the night.

More severe forms of eczema will take longer to heal than milder symptoms, and parents need to be patient with the healing process. It may take months to recover. The amelioration of symptoms is a gradual and sometimes slow process, and the course of treatment often has ups and downs, including flare-ups in response to specific or unidentified stressors. Parents of children with more severe symptoms may be frustrated with the persistent itching and slow progress of recovery. Fortunately, natural treatments exist that can help to relieve the itching. During the course of treatment, babies may need an occasional dose of Benadryl (diphenhydramine) to relieve itching or an application of hydrocortisone to calm the inflammation. Remember that the goal for eczema is cure—the complete eradication of symptoms. This often requires healing the injured intestinal lining, which takes time. Babies may also be continually exposed to the allergens or irritants that aggravate their symptoms, and this continuous stimulation of skin reactions may be unavoidable. Some babies just have sensitive, reactive skin that is easily irritated by environmental factors or many foods. These babies will improve as the immune system becomes less reactive with holistic treatment.

---

summary

Although most parents have been told there is little that can be done for eczema beyond applying steroid or other nonsteroidal suppressive creams, we have seen in this chapter that a holistic perspective can actually cure this condition. In subsequent chapters, I'll address other allergic problems, including asthma and chronic congestion, that often accompany eczema. In fact, all of these problems have a similar cause, and the emphasis in treatment is to rebalance and improve the impaired immune function. In chapter 8 you will find a detailed discussion of the fundamental principles involved in treating this immune-system dysfunction.

CHAPTER 4

- - - - - - - - - - - -

fevers: the good fight

Why talk about fevers? Few things scare parents more than a fever in their babies. How could such a scary experience possibly be good? Because without fevers we would all succumb to infections. When animals are deprived of the ability to fight infections with a fever, they die. Fevers fight infections. Fevers are nature's healing response. They should not be suppressed. A fever speeds up metabolism and heart rate, increasing blood circulation. It increases white blood cell production to fight bacteria and viruses, and it increases production of interferon, a natural antiviral chemical in the body. Babies get fevers to exercise their immune systems so they can build their own immunity to the pathogenic microbes they encounter. For all of these reasons, fevers represent a healing process and a healthy body defense. Fevers comprise the body's "good fight" in its effort to ward off pathogens.

what is a fever?

A *fever* is a temperature above 100.5° F (38° C). Anything below that is just a normal variation in temperature. Fever is caused by the white blood cells' response to invasion by pathogens, viruses, or bacteria. The white blood cells then release the chemical pyrogen, which stimulates the hypothalamus in the brain to turn up the body's thermostat.

Fever is often accompanied by discomfort and other symptoms, and these can be treated. A fever with localized symptoms such as runny nose, ear pain, or diarrhea is less worrisome than a fever without other apparent causes. However, many illnesses in babies begin with a fever as the first sign, signaling that the body is mounting an immune response. Then other symptoms may appear in the next day or two. It is always reassuring to know what is causing a fever because babies who have no obvious focus of infection may be harboring a more serious internal infection. Whenever your baby has a fever, careful surveillance and communication with your baby's health care provider are important. One of the most common causes of fever in babies is *roseola*, a viral illness characterized by a high fever up to 105° F (40.5° C) that lasts for several days without other symptoms. Then babies get a rash, and the illness is over. Most babies have roseola once and then develop permanent immunity to the virus.

Some babies develop a fever much more readily than others. With every virus they will get hot. Some of them feel like they are little toaster ovens on full broil. Some will seem to get a fever at any opportunity. Other babies get fevers that come and go repeatedly for days on end. And sometimes a fever and fussiness will be the only symptoms of an illness. Then there are babies who only get cold symptoms but seldom have a fever. Some babies run a temperature when they're teething. Although teething itself does not cause fevers, teething phases do seem to coincide with small illnesses, and your baby may get fevers and infections more readily at this time.

taking your baby's temperature

Babies get high fevers easily. They are naturally hot and reactive, quick responders with vigorous reactions. But most fevers aren't dangerous. Brain damage occurs if the body temperature rises to 108° F (42° C), but the body has very good mechanisms for keeping the temperature under 106° F (41° C).

Moms and dads are very good at telling how hot their babies are from touch. And the temperature goes up and down over the course of an illness and throughout the day and night, making the temperature reading not a very good indicator of the severity of the illness. Keep these variables in mind when evaluating your baby's temperature. If you want to know your baby's temperature to reassure yourself or to see if she does have a fever, then get a forehead thermometer that scans the temperature of the temporal artery, available at most drug stores. Slide the scanner across your baby's forehead and—bingo. It calculates the temperature of the blood and displays it on a small screen.

danger signs

Fevers in themselves are not dangerous to babies, but a persistent fever may be an indication of an infection that warrants professional evaluation and treatment. Whenever there is no apparent cause of a fever, it is worrisome if the fever persists for more than a day. A persistent fever does not necessarily indicate a serious disease, but getting the opinion of a medical professional is prudent. Vomiting in a baby with a fever is always a cause for concern, since vomiting frequently occurs in meningitis (a serious infection of the spinal cord and brain). It is wise to closely observe a baby who is vomiting. If accompanied by listlessness and difficulty waking your baby, then there is even more concern and the baby should see a doctor.

Any baby under three months of age with a fever should be seen by a doctor. Infants do not have the ability to fight off infections on their own, and even a simple infection can quickly develop into a serious, invasive illness. In infants, the cause of an infection may not be visible through symptoms. Bladder infections are fairly common at this age, and doctors may want to do lab tests to look for more invasive illness if your newborn has a fever.

With any illness, the most important indicator of the need for medical care is your baby's level of energy, not the level of fever. A baby who appears weak and lethargic and who has little energy to cry and nurse may have a worrisome condition. A screaming baby may have pain with an illness, but that level of energy indicates a robust reaction. Babies who are weak may not be fighting off an illness adequately.

If a fever persists for more than two days, call your baby's health care provider. If a cold or cough has been occurring for several days and your baby then gets a fever, this may be a sign that her immune system is not managing the infection well on its own. A deeper infection can take hold in these circumstances. Have your baby see a professional in this situation too. And at any point in an illness, if your baby seems very sleepy and unresponsive to stimulation or weak and unable to generate that lusty crying, get a professional's opinion.

Again, *any* fever in a baby under three months of age should be evaluated by a medical professional.

febrile seizures

Seizures can occur with fevers (these convulsions are called *febrile seizures*). Usually these will occur on the first day of a fever, before any other worrisome signs appear. Febrile seizures are actually fairly common. According to the National Institute of Neurological Disorders and Stroke (2009), 4 percent of young children have at least one. These seizures are frightening to parents, but they are harmless to children. They do not cause brain damage or any subsequent learning problems, and children who have had febrile seizures seldom develop epilepsy later in life. Only 2 to 5 percent of children who have a febrile seizure will go on to develop epilepsy (National Institute of Neurological Disorders and Stroke 2009).

If your baby begins twitching or jerking with a fever, stay calm, turn your baby on her side, and do not restrain her. Time the seizure. If it lasts more than five minutes or if the baby becomes unconscious, call 911. Seizures usually last for a few seconds or up to five minutes. This amount of time will seem like an eternity when you're watching a seizure, but it's normal. Other accompanying symptoms may include vomiting, a rolling back of the eyes, or loss of consciousness. There is no reason to go to an emergency room or call 911 if your baby has a short seizure with a fever and remain conscious. After the seizure is over, call your doctor to see if an exam is needed to discover any other causes, such as meningitis. Giving fever-reducing drugs does not prevent febrile seizures.

treatment of fevers

Treating your baby's fever and acute symptoms at home is easy enough. The goal of treatment is to encourage healing and stimulate a strong immune response. Reducing the fever is not the goal, as the fever will do what is necessary to fight the illness. Natural remedies will encourage the fight.

The first and easiest remedy to try is homeopathic *Belladonna*. The classical indications for *Belladonna* are fever with sudden onset, radiating heat, and flushing and redness of the skin. There may be redness (indicating inflammation) at some specific location in the body: in the throat, the ears, the eyes, the skin—pretty much anywhere. Older children will complain of a headache. Babies who need *Belladonna* are often quiet and subdued, moaning and very hot to touch. Or they may be crying with discomfort. *Belladonna* is indicated before significant discharge develops with a cold or other symptoms appear later in an illness that would point the way to another remedy. For indications in the homeopathic treatment of colds, see chapter 5, and for medicines that treat other specific types of infections, see my book *Child Health Guide*.

If babies are very uncomfortable and screaming in apparent pain, then you may want to try giving homeopathic *Chamomilla*. Often one dose will calm your baby and allow her to get back to sleep.

Giving herbs for immune-system support is always indicated. Echinacea and black elderberry are usually well tolerated by babies, and children's liquid extract preparations are available at most health-food stores. Yin Chao Junior (Health Concerns) is a Chinese herbal formula available through any licensed health care practitioner and is indicated for the first stage of an illness. Yin Chao is a formula developed in 1798 to disperse Wind Heat and relieve Heat in acute illness caused by external pathogens. Windbreaker (Chinese Medicine Works) is a pediatric formula with similar therapeutic effect that also clears Phlegm.

Sponging babies off with a cool cloth may momentarily relieve discomfort as the water evaporates from the skin. But sponging does not reduce fevers because the body's thermostat is unaffected by external manipulation of the temperature. Never put alcohol on a baby to accomplish this, as it will be absorbed through the skin.

Cautions Regarding Drugs for Fever

It is best to avoid the use of Tylenol (acetaminophen) and Advil (ibuprofen). Certainly parents should not reach for these drugs at the first sign of fever. There may be times when babies need some relief from pain, and a dose of ibuprofen may provide a good night's sleep in a truly distressed baby. But these drugs should not be given in a cavalier fashion, and homeopathic medicines usually accomplish the same functions without any risk of side effects. Here are some cautions about fever-reducing drugs. They do carry some potential risks.

Acetaminophen

Acetaminophen (Tylenol) is not the best choice of drugs for babies. Acetaminophen is potentially toxic to the liver. In one case-review study, poisoning with acetaminophen proved to be the number one cause of acute liver failure (Larson et al. 2005). Although most of the cases occurred with high doses of acetaminophen, even a daily dose as low as 1.2 grams (2.5 Extra Strength Tylenol) resulted in acute liver failure in some cases in adults (the equivalent of 160 mg in a twenty-pound baby). Of those cases of acute liver failure from acetaminophen, 29 percent died. Because babies have relatively undeveloped livers, they are at least three times more susceptible to the adverse effects of drugs like Tylenol.

It also seems that suppressing fever with acetaminophen increases the length of viral illnesses. In one study of the flu, giving Tylenol during the illness to reduce fever was associated with an average of nine days of symptoms compared to about five days of symptoms in the untreated group (Plaisance et al. 2000). Suppressing fevers with acetaminophen in the first year of life may also increase the risk of allergies, eczema, and asthma in later childhood, according to a study in the British medical journal *Lancet* (Beasley 2008).

Ibuprofen

Ibuprofen (Advil, Motrin) also has some attendant risks. Though it is a better choice than acetaminophen for relief of pain, you should also use caution and be circumspect about overuse and routine use of ibuprofen.

Ibuprofen can cause a relatively rare reaction called *Stevens-Johnson syndrome*. This is a serious and sometimes fatal skin disease that occurs as an allergic drug reaction to ibuprofen and other medications. The disease begins with flu-like symptoms and progresses to inflammation of mucous membranes and blistering eruptions on the skin. It then causes the detachment of large areas of skin. If the disease continues, it can prove fatal due to loss of skin, infections, and damage to major organs such as the heart or lungs.

Aspirin

Aspirin should never be given to children with fevers. Aspirin given during a viral illness can cause Reye's syndrome, severe liver dysfunction, and brain swelling. Symptoms include repeated vomiting, lethargy, delirium, seizures, and coma. With other, safer options available to you, don't keep aspirin at home.

- -

prevention of progression of illness

When your baby is showing signs of illness with a fever you may want to start giving immune-system activators that will help to prevent serious illness. The single herbs echinacea and black elderberry stimulate the immune response. Homeopathic medicines like *Belladonna* have a mitigating effect on illness severity. And Chinese herbal formulas like Yin Chao and Windbreaker have appropriate combinations of herbs that can be used during the

first days of an illness to assist the body's own healing mecha‑
nisms. All of these simple interventions will help to keep fevers
and discomfort at reasonable levels and gently speed the illness
along to recovery, preventing complications.

- -
summary

Fevers are a healthy response to invasion by pathogens, and it is
best not to suppress a fever with drugs. For most fevers, watch‑
ful waiting using home remedies is an appropriate first response,
with the idea of consulting your baby's medical provider if a fever
persists. All babies under three months of age with a fever need
to see a doctor because of their relative inability to fight off infec‑
tions on their own, but older babies will usually develop fevers as
a natural and normal healing response. Using gentle treatment
for the illness as discussed in this and the following chapters is
a good first step before contacting your baby's doctor. Of course,
if you are concerned about your baby looking sick or developing
symptoms that you don't understand, then give your doctor a call
for reassurance and guidance.

CHAPTER 5

----

colds and other
simple illnesses

If this is your first baby, then he's probably not getting sick often. Babies who stay at home don't have much exposure to the illnesses that spread around in the winter months. Add to this the fact that your baby has acquired all of Mom's antibodies from the shared bloodstream in utero. Babies are protected from any pathogens (the viruses and bacteria associated with contagious disease) that their mothers have encountered in the past. There are always new strains of viruses, and your baby can catch one of these. But for the first six months your baby will likely avoid common bugs.

---

vulnerability factors

An exception is if there is more than one child in the home, especially toddlers. These older siblings tend to catch bugs from other children and bring them home to your family. And if your baby is in day care, then he will probably catch colds that are going around. Babies in any of these situations need all the help they can get.

By six months your baby may start getting colds. If he is born in the middle of the winter and his six-month birthday comes during the warm summer weather, then he might escape the onset of colds until fall or winter. Whatever the situation, by the end of his first year your baby is likely to catch some colds.

If this is your second or third baby, then an additional factor comes into play. Multiple pregnancies, breastfeeding, staying up at night with a crying baby, and taking care of a growing family all take their toll on Mom's energy supplies. Being a mother is exacting and exhausting. Your storehouse of energy becomes depleted, and in the understanding of Chinese medicine, subsequent babies are often born with depleted Prenatal Qi. This will then be reflected in deficient Wei Qi, the protective energetic level of the body that defends your baby against external pathogens. In Western terms, these babies tend to have weakened immune systems, with a greater tendency to develop recurrent acute illnesses, adverse reactions to vaccinations, and allergies. Remember that the term "acute illness" refers to a self-limited condition that will resolve, and the term "chronic illness" refers to symptoms that tend to persist over time.

Whatever the cause, if your baby gets sick or has repeated illnesses or chronic respiratory symptoms, there are very effective means within holistic medicine to treat the problem. This strategy may include relieving the symptoms of acute illness or overcoming chronic symptoms. In either case, the holistic model focuses on building the strength of the immune system.

The Holistic Baby Guide applies to illnesses that your baby is likely to experience during the first year. For a more complete description of home treatment for a wide range of acute illnesses that older children contract on a regular basis, see my book *Child Health Guide*.

colds and coughs

The most common symptoms during the first year of life are runny and stuffy noses accompanied by fussiness. These symptoms then sometimes progress into coughing. Parents learn to dread the onset of runny noses because it means weeks of sniffling, coughing, and misery. But it doesn't need to be that way. With holistic care, colds will go away quickly and occur infrequently.

It is important for babies to get colds. These illnesses exercise the immune system and develop the antibodies that will recognize and fight off viruses in the future. Colds merely represent a necessary and perhaps unpleasant episode of growing up. Just be aware that your baby will be stronger as a result of getting these simple respiratory infections.

Not all stuffy noses are actually caused by a cold virus. Some infants tend to have stuffy noses a lot, especially when lying down. The congestion may make nursing difficult. This is just a case of small nasal passages and a tendency to produce Phlegm. Sometimes a simple homeopathic medicine like *Pulsatilla* will help. Saline nasal spray or a few drops of salt water in your baby's nose can help temporarily. Taking your baby into a steamy bathroom with the shower on can serve the same purpose.

Treatment of Colds

As soon as cold symptoms begin with a runny nose, you can start a program to encourage the body's healing response. An

active response to cold symptoms at their onset will cut these illnesses short. The two Western herbs that have proven most effective are echinacea and black elderberry. Both of these are prepared
in pediatric extract form by various manufacturers.

Chinese Herbs

Chinese herbs are appropriate as well. Yin Chao is a classic
Chinese formula that dispels Heat and helps the body fight off
the attack of external pathogens. Health Concerns makes Yin
Chao Junior in a liquid extract. Another liquid pediatric formula,
Windbreaker (CMW) clears Wind, Heat, and Phlegm, relieving
the signs and symptoms of acute invasion by external pathogenic
influences. Dr. Jake's Children's Cold Away (Yin Qiao Gan Mao
Wan) combines Yin Chiao with another formula, Gan Mao Ling,
to treat the early stage of cold or flu with symptoms of sore throat,
low fever, headache, swollen glands, dry cough, nasal discharge
or congestion, general aching, and swollen lymph glands. The
formula clears Heat, dispels Wind, benefits the throat, opens the
nasal passages, relieves cough, and diffuses Lung Qi.

Several pharmacies make Xiao Chai Hu Tang (Minor
Bupleurum) in powder or granular form. This formula is especially
suited for colds that have continued for a few days or for congestion that persists following a cold. Blue Poppy makes a liquid pediatric formula called CQ Junior, which combines Minor Bupleurum
and Yin Qiao. All of these formulas are safe for babies.

Homeopathy

Homeopathic medicines are gentle and simple to use. For the
first stage of a cold, including a runny nose with clear mucus,
begin with *Allium cepa*. If the cold progresses to thicker mucus,
then switch to *Pulsatilla*. If a fever accompanies the cold symptoms, you may want to consider *Belladonna* for the first stage of a

respiratory infection. The 12 or 30 strength (designated either x or c) is usually available in pellet form at health-food stores. Even newborn babies can take homeopathic medicines. Just grind the pellets and dissolve in water or breast milk. Typical dosage is three times per day until symptoms improve.

Prevention of Complications Due to Colds

The most important issue in prevention is to make sure that simple colds do not progress into more serious or complicated illness. The best way to accomplish this is to maintain a strong and resilient immune system. The discussions in chapter 8 provide a detailed view of immune system repair and maintenance. For otherwise healthy children, providing some simple supplements such as colostrum and vitamin D3 (cholecalciferol), as I discussed in chapter 3, will boost immune function and prevent inflammatory reactions. Using the herbal treatments described in this chapter will be especially effective in preventing more serious disease processes from taking hold.

Treatment of Coughs

Coughs are harder to treat because they can be caused by many different physiological and disease processes, and the treatment will vary accordingly. Most coughs in babies are caused by mucus that collects in the throat, which wakes them in the night and sounds loose in the morning when they try to clear it. Irritation in the throat and upper airways can also cause coughing. These types of coughs sound throaty. This may be accompanied by a rattling sound when your baby breathes, caused by air moving through this thick mucus in the throat. A dry, barking cough may indicate that your baby has *croup*, a viral illness that causes swelling and constriction in the throat. Croup is characterized by a cough that sounds like a seal's bark, but it can also cause difficulty breathing from the constriction of the airway.

Coughs can also be caused by problems in the airways of the chest or in the lungs. When you or a doctor listens to your baby's chest, there may be sounds that indicate mucus in these airways. This is the province of medical treatment and consultation with your child's health care provider, but even coughs in the chest indicative of bronchitis or even pneumonia can benefit from holistic methods. Coughing in babies is cause for concern and a good reason to get a diagnosis from your doctor. However, even babies who need antibiotics or other medications for these symptoms will also benefit from holistic care.

Persistent or severe episodes of coughing in babies under a year of age are generally not the realm for home remedy care for two reasons. First, treating a cough takes some prescribing skill. And second, coughs in babies may be an indication of a condition that requires professional medical care. Of course, a simple cough that accompanies a cold can be treated at home. But if your baby is lethargic or develops a fever with a cough, then a doctor's exam is indicated to make sure your baby doesn't have a serious infection that could worsen.

Conventional cough syrups are ineffective and should never be used with babies. They also have significant side effects. They have no place in the treatment of children (Paul et al. 2004). Decongestants have been associated with accidental and tragic infant deaths, and they should also never be given to babies (Rimsza and Newberry 2008).

Chinese Herbs

There are several soothing Chinese liquid herbal cough formulas appropriate for babies and available through Chinese herbalists and health-food stores. Dr. Jake's Pediatric Lung Clear Formula (Xiao Er Zi Qing Fei Tang) treats cough, bronchitis, whooping cough, and croup. This formula addresses the early stages of common acute cough presentations, including cough due to Lung Fire, copious Phlegm Heat, or sticky Phlegm Heat.

Fritillária and Pinellia Syrup by Golden Flower treats loose-sounding productive coughs with lots of phlegm. Fritillary is one of the primary Chinese herbs for cough. Several forms of cough syrup incorporate fritillary with other herbs to relieve coughs and phlegm in children. Beware of formulas that contain honey, which should not be given to babies under twelve months old, and do not use syrups that contain preservatives such as methylparaben.

Two liquid pediatric herbal formulas by Chinese Medicine Works address coughing. Chest Relief is a formula that treats cough by subduing the cough, dispelling phlegm, moistening dryness, soothing the throat, and relaxing the mind. Pipe Cleaner has more decongesting properties and can be used for cases with more chest congestion with coughing. This formula fits coughs with a deeper sound and mucus in the chest, which may be diagnosed as bronchitis or pneumonia by your child's doctor

Lung Qi Jr., a pediatric herbal formula available from Blue Poppy Herbs, has the qualities of relieving Phlegm Heat and coughing in children, especially when they have a tendency to catch colds repeatedly.

Homeopathy

Homeopathy provides excellent treatment for coughs, but the decision to use one medicine over others depends upon some fine distinctions and discrimination in prescribing. This makes it difficult to treat coughs at home. A short description of several homeopathic cough medicines follows. I have arbitrarily separated coughing into dry- and wet- or loose-sounding coughs because that is how your baby will sound to you, but in actuality most homeopathic medicines can be prescribed for either type of cough. The distinctions to a lay person may seem complex and confusing. That is why homeopathic prescribing requires a great deal of training and experience. These coughs may accompany several diagnostic categories, including chest colds, bronchitis, flu, pneumonia, bronchiolitis, or asthma (see also chapter 7 on asthma).

Dry Cough

This is a cough that sounds dry and tight. The dry cough won't sound wet or mucousy.

- *Bryonia.* The coughing that indicates *Bryonia* as the correct medicine is provoked by any motion of the body. It tends to be worse in a warm room and better in the open air. Children who need *Bryonia* are usually very thirsty and may be feverish. The cough seems painful.

- *Spongia.* Coughing that indicates *Spongia* is hard and dry with a hoarse voice. This barking, croupy cough sounds like a seal. The cough is better from eating, drinking, or nursing.

- *Kali carbonicum.* Children who need *Kali carbonicum* must sit up and lean forward in order to breathe more easily. They characteristically wake at two to three a.m. with a dry cough. They must have open air when an attack occurs, but their cough is often brought on by cold weather.

Loose Cough

This cough sounds wet and is characterized by mucus production.

- *Kali bichromicum.* The coughing that indicates *Kali bichromicum* comes primarily from the throat irritation of postnasal drainage, but there seems to be a lot of phlegm. This may choke babies and make it difficult for them to nurse. The phlegm and congestion may be present in the nose as well, and parents may see thick, green nasal discharge. Or the congestion may be stuck in the nose and sinuses and not visible at all.

- **Ipecacuanha.** *Ipecacuanha* is the appropriate medicine for symptoms characterized by racking, rattling coughs with rumbling in the chest, often accompanied by wheezing sounds. Children who need this medicine will cough with every breath and may have gagging or vomiting from the coughing attacks. These attacks occur in warm or damp weather, and symptoms are better in the open air and worse when lying down. Mucus collects in the throat or chest, causing a loose, gagging cough. Loud, rough, and rumbling noises from the congestion can be heard in the chest on breathing.

- **Antimonium tartaricum.** The cough that indicates *Antimonium tartaricum* is characterized by a great deal of mucus in the chest, with very little expectorated. Children who require this medicine seem weak and wheezy. This is a worrisome-sounding cough. These children seem sicker than those who need *Ipecacuanha*, though the coughs that indicate *Ipecacuanha* may have more rumbling chest sounds. Children who need *Antimonium tartaricum* must sit up to breathe. The chest rattles and the cough is loose and worse in the evening and at night. This is the cough that is always diagnosed as bronchitis or pneumonia.

Prevention of Complications Due to Coughs

The same issues discussed in the previous section about preventing colds from worsening will apply to chest colds and coughs. Children who have a resilient immune system will usually recover quickly from coughs that accompany respiratory infections.

persistent congestion and sinus infections

It may seem like your baby is constantly congested or he has colds that last forever. Or your pediatrician may have told you that your baby has a sinus infection. Persistent stuffy or snotty noses or snoring are all too frequent in the first year of life and in toddlers. Green mucus from your baby's nose and difficulty nursing because of a clogged nose are disconcerting symptoms.

Babies tend to get Damp conditions. In Chinese medicine, Dampness and Phlegm occur when fluids and Qi become stagnant. Often this process begins in a weakened or disordered digestive system, which is responsible for sending nutrients to the rest of the body. If Stomach Qi is weak, a cascade of disorders can begin from lack of Nutritive Qi production by the digestive tract, leading to susceptibility to illness and stagnations of Qi with Dampness. If the digestive system is not providing adequate nutrition, then the lungs will not be nourished, and they cannot generate Qi. As a result, the respiratory tract will develop stagnation, Dampness, and inflammation. This process is so common that many Chinese herbal formulas have been developed to address this dynamic, the imbalance of Stomach/Spleen (digestive) and Lung systems.

Functional medicine has developed a method for assessing and addressing these same issues from a Western medical perspective. If you normalize digestive function, the immune system will recover. This will calm inflammation and decrease the generation of excess mucus.

In the meantime, the sinuses may in fact be congested. Your baby may have inflamed mucous membranes and even bacterial overgrowth with a sinus infection. These symptoms will need to be addressed at the same time that you build healthy immune mechanisms. The best ways to treat chronic congestion directly in babies is through homeopathic medicines and Chinese herbs. Then you can prevent recurrences by addressing any underlying digestive problems, activating the immune system through direct stimulation with supplements, treating constitutional weakness, and boosting deficient Qi. We will explore the methodology for doing so in more detail in chapter 8.

Sinus infections in children do not usually require antibiotic treatment. In fact, antibiotics will often worsen the problem because of their disrupting effect on the immune system. The result will be recurrences of infections, more inflammation, and further exacerbation of sinus congestion. A much better approach lies in the methods of holistic practice.

Treatment of Congestion

Holistic medicine offers many effective ways of treating your baby's congestion.

Homeopathy

Homeopathic medicines for congestion in babies are simple to use. Start with a 12 or 30 potency of the medicine and repeat it once or twice a day until the symptoms improve.

If an infant has persistent stuffiness without other symptoms, the first medicine to try is *Sambucus*. This is not to be confused with the syrup of black elderberry that is used for colds and flus sold under the trade name Sambucol. *Sambucus* is a classic homeopathic remedy for "snuffly" newborns and young babies with dryness and no apparent discharge.

When congestion follows a cold and persists after the acute phase is over, or if you suspect a sinus infection, then give *Kali bichromicum*. This medicine treats congestion with thick discharges that may be greenish. Babies who need *Kali bichromicum* are often worse when lying down because the mucus drains into their throats and they may gag on it or try to cough it out.

Chinese Herbs

Chinese herbal formulas will focus on Dampness, Phlegm, and strengthening and moving Stomach and Spleen Qi. It's hard to get away from the concept of Stomach/Spleen deficiency and stagnation in babies because so much of their energy is focused on digestion and because their digestive tracts are immature and sensitive to upsetting influences and stresses such as nursing problems and inappropriate introduction of solids. The classic formula for these symptoms is Minor Bupleurum (Xiao Chai Hu Tang), which addresses the Liver-Spleen disharmony common to infants. The relative Liver excess and Spleen deficiency leads to stagnation, Dampness, and congestion.

Other formulas include Head Clear (CMW), which addresses and eliminates Dampness, Phlegm, and congestion while strengthening the Stomach and Lung and the body's resistance (Wei Qi) to external pathogens.

Prevention of Chronic Congestion and Sinus Infections

Again, the best preventive for the development of persistent congestion is to maintain a strong immune system and a healthy, balanced digestive tract. As we have seen, immune function and digestive health are intimately connected. Methods for helping your baby maintain a resilient immune system will be found in chapter 8. Treating colds with an appropriate anti-inflammatory and decongesting protocol as described in the previous sections will also help to prevent a downward spiral into chronic sinus problems and persistent stuffiness in your baby.

GI bugs: vomiting and diarrhea

Sooner or later your baby will develop a gastrointestinal virus with vomiting and diarrhea. Fortunately, these symptoms are easy to treat.

Most acute diarrhea episodes with fever in children are caused by rotavirus, and most children acquire a rotavirus infection by the time they are five years old. The illness usually begins with a fever and vomiting, followed by four to eight days of diarrhea. Sometimes the diarrhea is profuse, in which case there is a danger of dehydration. Because there are different strains of the virus, children can have the illness more than once, though the first infection is usually the worst.

Other, less common causes of acute diarrhea include bacterial infection, food poisoning, and intestinal parasites. In these situations, other family members are likely to have symptoms. Diarrhea caused by parasites is usually attributed to *protozoa* (small organisms living in the gut). These can be acquired through contaminated water, often during foreign travel or camping trips. A child with persistent diarrhea can easily be tested for these causes.

Diarrhea from rotavirus infection is *self-limited*—it will eventually resolve itself. The real danger from diarrhea is fluid loss and dehydration. The primary symptom of dehydration is weight loss of 3 to 9 percent of body weight. A weight loss greater than 9 percent of body weight indicates severe dehydration. If your baby is not losing weight, then dehydration is unlikely. Other symptoms include dry mouth and skin, lack of urine output, sunken eyes, and lethargy (difficulty staying awake). Dehydration occurs because cells lining the intestine secrete salts. Due to the process of osmosis, water follows these minerals out of the body. Giving solutions of water with salts and sugar will cause water to be reabsorbed by the intestinal wall. (See "Treatment" for a recipe.)

If your baby has persistent diarrhea without a fever, then he likely has something other than an acute virus or other infection. Dietary causes of diarrhea are usually attributed to too much fruit or fruit juice or sensitivities to certain foods in the diet. Teething can be associated with diarrhea, or more serious chronic diseases can be the cause. Your medical provider is the best resource when diarrhea persists.

Danger Signs

If your newborn develops watery stools or bad-smelling stools, contact your doctor. Bloody stools at any time warrant a trip to the doctor. You should also consult your doctor if your baby is experiencing severe abdominal pain, lethargy, persistent diarrhea without signs of improvement, or vomiting that lasts more than twenty-four hours.

Treatment of GI Bugs

Try to make sure that your baby is drinking. Breast milk is the best fluid replacement for your baby. If your baby is no longer breastfeeding, then offer water. Babies with vomiting will tend to vomit anything put into their stomachs. Give only sips at a time, or offer your baby chips of ice or frozen fruit juice to avoid getting too much in the stomach at once. Babies need about 2.5 ounces of liquid per pound of body weight daily, so a fifteen-pound baby will need about 37 ounces of liquid. Of course, a sick baby may not take that much during the initial stage of an illness, but over the course of a week your baby will need to resume drinking to prevent dehydration.

If you suspect that your baby is dehydrated or if you want to prevent it, a rehydration fluid that contains salt and sugar will work best to replace fluid loss. You can make a simple rehydration fluid from the recipe below or use a commercial preparation like

Pedialyte. Give a small amount at a time, usually by the teaspoon. Do not use bottles, which may get clogged. Try to give one-fourth to one-half cup per feeding. Avoid fruit juices, which tend to make diarrhea worse. Give older babies bananas and avoid other raw fruits, which can aggravate diarrhea. Dehydration is a potentially serious situation that may require replacement of fluids by IV. A call to your doctor is warranted if you think your baby may be dehydrated.

---

homemade rehydration electrolyte solution

1 quart clean water

½ teaspoon table salt

½ teaspoon baking soda

8 teaspoons sugar

Homeopathy

Homeopathic treatment is straightforward. Homeopathic medicines are safe and can be used in even the youngest of infants. The most commonly indicated medicine for the first stage of vomiting and diarrhea is *Arsenicum album*. Symptoms that correspond to *Arsenicum* often begin in the middle of the night with vomiting, but this remedy can be used at the onset of any GI bug.

The other commonly indicated medicine is *Podophyllum*, which corresponds to profuse, watery, smelly stools that fill the diaper. The baby who needs *Podophyllum* will often have noisy, spluttering, explosive diarrhea. *Podophyllum* is often indicated for babies after symptoms have been present for a few days.

A third medicine for later stages and more serious cases of diarrhea is *Veratrum album*. This remedy fits the child who has become exhausted from the diarrhea and appears cold and sweaty. Stools are profuse and watery, and they may be accompanied by painful cramping and vomiting.

If your baby has repeated vomiting with a stomach bug, then try using homeopathic *Ipecacuanha*. This remedy will usually stop vomiting.

Probiotics

The other effective treatment for acute rotavirus infection in children is a probiotic supplement. The most consistently effective probiotic in pediatric clinical studies of rotavirus infections is *Lactobacillus rhamnosus* GG (Szajewska and Mrukowicz 2001). Other probiotic strains that have proven effective for children with diarrhea are *Saccharomyces boulardii* and *Lactobacillus reuteri*. To be effective, these need to be given in a high enough potency, at least 10 billion per day (Guandalini 2008). Combinations of probiotic strains including *Streptococcus thermophilus, Lactobacillus acidophilus*, and *Bifidobacterium bifidum* have also been shown to be effective in reducing the duration of children's diarrhea (Canani et al. 2007).

Prevention of Complications Due to GI Bugs

Maintaining healthy digestive function in your baby by providing a supplement of probiotics is likely to prevent serious intestinal symptoms with these GI bugs. The more resilience your baby has to ward off viruses and bacteria with a vigorous immune response, the less likely he will be to suffer from prolonged illnesses or their complications.

summary

This chapter should provide you with most of the tools you will need to get through the common bugs your baby might acquire in the first year or two. Dealing with a sick baby is never fun, but it can be relatively straightforward if you have the right tools to manage the symptoms, keep your baby comfortable, and prevent complications of these simple illnesses. Apply the holistic methods in this chapter and you will find that most of these illnesses resolve pretty readily. And soon, you too will be an expert at getting your baby through these rough times with a minimal amount of discomfort.

CHAPTER 6

- - - - - - - - - - -

ear problems

It is unfortunate that your baby can easily develop recurrent and chronic ear problems. At about six months, babies lose the maternal antibodies that protected them from common viral and bacterial infections. After that age they become susceptible, and they need to develop their own antibodies to these pathogens. If one of these viruses or bacteria happens to cause an ear infection, then your pediatrician may prescribe antibiotics. This is often the beginning of recurrent ear problems. Continuing to treat the fluid that collects in the middle ear or repeated red eardrums with more antibiotics just exacerbates the problem. And sometimes babies will have these ear problems even if they don't get antibiotics. In this chapter you will learn the reasons that these ear problems tend to plague babies and find out how to cure them.

the middle ear

Behind the eardrum lies a tiny cavity within the bones of the skull that is filled with air. This is the middle ear. It contains three small bones that transfer sound from the movement of the eardrum (the *tympanic membrane*) to the inner ear, where nerve fibers detect these movements and communicate them to the brain. The brain then translates them into intelligible sounds. This little miracle depends upon a happy and functional middle ear. If all goes well, this apparatus works unhindered and without mishap.

The proper function of the eardrum and the transfer of sound by the bones of the middle ear depend upon the presence of air in the middle-ear cavity. This air is provided by the auditory tube, most commonly known as the *Eustachian tube* (after a sixteenth-century anatomist, Bartolomeo Eustachi). This tube connects the middle-ear cavity with the throat. It remains closed most of the time and opens with a small click during swallowing. The swallowing motion pumps air into the middle ear. The Eustachian tube also drains any fluid from the middle ear, such as liquid that may collect there during a cold.

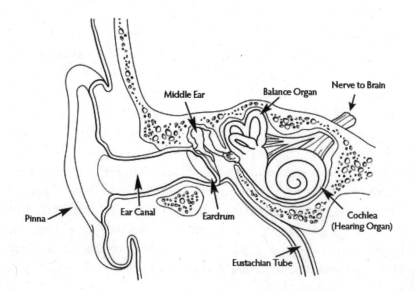

In babies, the Eustachian tube does not tend to work so well. The pumping action of the tube depends upon a series of contractions of small muscles attached to the tube. Like other muscles in a baby's body, their coordination tends to develop gradually over time. The Eustachian tube works better in older children than in infants and toddlers. If the Eustachian tube does not open consistently, then the mucous membranes that line the middle ear will use up the oxygen in the cavity and create a partial vacuum relative to the air pressure on the outside of the eardrum. This negative pressure pulls on the eardrum, making it less pliable and responsive to the movement of sound waves. This can diminish hearing. The mucous membranes that line the middle ear can also secrete mucus during a respiratory infection, and this fluid can collect there if the Eustachian tube is not draining the middle ear effectively. This fluid will tend to press against the eardrum, impairing its ability to move well and again diminishing hearing. Fluid in the middle ear can also become a breeding ground for bacteria, resulting in infections and more mucus production, compounding the problem.

When babies have colds the eardrum tends to get inflamed, along with the membranes of the nose and throat. Sometimes this inflammation in the middle ear results in pain because the eardrum has many nerve endings and tends to be exquisitely sensitive. Some doctors who look at the eardrum and see that it's red may be quick to prescribe antibiotics for what is interpreted as an ear infection (known as *otitis media*). But antibiotics tend to cause problems.

Antibiotics kill off the beneficial bacteria in the body, making babies more prone to infections. Billions of bacteria in the body coexist in a harmonious balance. There are more bacteria in and on the surface of our bodies than the total of human cells in our bodies. Many of these bacteria are protective, or they are essential for digesting food and extracting nutrients from food. Antibiotics destroy the protective bacteria of the intestines, allowing an overgrowth of harmful yeast and causing diarrhea because of bacterial disruption, and sometimes producing leaky gut syndrome. And antibiotics can also encourage bacteria to build up resistance to the antibiotics so that more serious infections may occur later. A more insidious effect of antibiotics is explained by Jake Fratkin, OMD, in his article "Pediatric Ear Infections and Chinese Medicine" (2004):

> ... Antibiotics also injure the production of white blood cells by destroying mitochondria. When an infection occurs normally, white blood cells multiply to help the body's immune response. Inflammation and mucus secretion [are] part of its natural mechanisms. When antibiotics inhibit ... WBC production, the body is slow to return to normalcy. This period of lowered immunity allows a reinfection. (This [destruction of the white blood cell response] is the reason why antibiotics seem to reduce sore throat, fever, and phlegm quickly, even when there is no bacterial infection.)

For these reasons, the American Academy of Pediatrics (2004) recommends that most children with acute ear infections can be observed for a period of forty-eight to seventy-two hours without antibiotics. This recommendation is based on the understanding from clinical studies that 61 percent of children with acute ear infections are better within twenty-four hours and 75 percent have complete resolution of symptoms within seven days without the use of antibiotics (Rosenfeld and Kay 2003).

Although the American Academy of Pediatrics recommendation suggests that clinicians take a wait-and-see attitude toward ear infections, they still advocate antibiotics for persistent symptoms. I do not recommend antibiotics for ear infections. They can nearly always be managed with holistic treatment, avoiding the many problems that antibiotics themselves create. Antibiotics are not an effective, safe, or appropriate first-line treatment for ear infections or other simple respiratory infections.

treatment of ear infections

When your baby is experiencing pain that may indicate an ear infection, you have a number of options to help her feel better. These include remedies you can use at home and getting the help of professional practitioners.

Home Treatment

Letting ear infections heal on their own is one way to approach them, but holistic care offers several effective options for treatment of the infection that will relieve pain and help to prevent the collection of fluid in the middle ear. Babies cry for a number of different reasons, pain being only one of them. But you will usually know if your baby has pain. Earaches can be excruciating to babies, and it's always good to know whether a child's ears are hurting. By six months of age your baby can indicate the source of pain by putting her hands to her ears with an earache or in her mouth if the pain is due to teething or a sore throat. Prior to that age, babies have no way to indicate the cause of the trouble.

You can use an inexpensive home otoscope to examine your child's ears yourself. These are simplified versions of the tools that doctors use to look in children's ears, and they are available through many online resources. A bit of practice when your baby is healthy will reveal a whitish gray eardrum. If you see red, then the discomfort your baby is experiencing may be coming from the ear. However, a pink or red eardrum does not necessarily mean there is an infection. It does mean there is some inflammation, but this often occurs when babies are fighting off a virus or even when they are crying.

Treatment for an earache is straightforward. If your baby is crying in pain, then a few drops of any type of cooking oil warmed to body temperature placed into the ear canal can be very soothing.

Homeopathy

Homeopathic medicines have proven to be very effective in clinical practice for relieving the symptoms of acute earaches. And several studies have documented the effectiveness of homeopathic treatment of acute ear infections. In one study, *Pulsatilla* was used in a double-blind, placebo-controlled trial of thirty-eight children with acute otitis. All cases in the treatment group were improved upon follow-up evaluation, compared to only 73 percent of the placebo group (Möessinger 1985).

Homeopathic medicines are chosen on the basis of the presenting symptoms. If your baby is very sensitive to the pain and to touching the ear and she's also very irritable, then the most commonly indicated remedy is *Hepar-sulph*. This can be administered in a 12 or 30 strength every few hours if needed. If your baby is more clingy, sad, and wanting attention, then *Pulsatilla* is more strongly indicated. There are other homeopathic medicines for ear infections that your practitioner might prescribe, but these two should suffice to get you through most earaches.

Chinese Herbs

Golden Flower Chinese Herbs makes an excellent Chinese herbal extract called Children's Ear Formula that can be prescribed by your practitioner. The formula, developed by Dr. Jake Fratkin and designed for acute ear infections, is extremely effective in resolving the symptoms quickly. This formula includes herbs that transform and drain Phlegm and clear Heat and toxins while relieving pain.

Prevention of Ear Infections

The best prevention of ear infections is to avoid the use of antibiotics and maintain a robust immune system by applying the principles and supplements discussed in chapter 8. Colds don't need to settle in babies' ears, and a baby with a resilient immune response should get through these illnesses without complicating infections.

---

repeated ear infections

Children who receive antibiotics for ear infections often proceed into a downward spiral of repeated ear infections and repeated courses of antibiotics. At least half of all ear infections are viral (that is, caused by a virus and therefore unaffected by antibiotics, which work on bacteria), and there is no way to determine whether symptoms are due to a virus or bacteria. In most situations, antibiotics will have little effect on the progress of symptoms, even when an infection is bacterial. The redness and inflammation of the eardrum often persists. In these cases, children are often prescribed several courses of different antibiotics, even if the discomfort disappears, which it tends to do on its own. Then the adverse effects of the antibiotics take their toll, setting up a situation of chronic infections and lowered resistance. It's very common to see babies who have one cold and ear infection after another during the winter months, with a resulting history of many prescriptions for antibiotics.

Getting Professional Help

Babies with recurrent ear problems also need an immune-system boost. Use a supplement program of probiotics to reestablish normal bacterial ecology, vitamin D3 (cholecalciferol) to support the immune system, colostrum to provide an immunological boost, and fish oil to prevent inflammation. Herbal supplements with astragalus and medicinal mushrooms will support long-term healthy immune function. *Astragalus* is a well-known herb for immune-system support. And the mushrooms shiitake, maitake, reishi, ganoderma, and others provide an activating and corrective influence on the immune system. All of these contain polysaccharides (long-chain sugars) that encourage the body's resistance to infection by pathogens. Resilience (CMW) is an excellent liquid formulation of astragalus and mushrooms. See chapter 8 for a complete discussion of immune-system supplementation. There may be other factors such as digestive problems, allergies, or chronic congestion that also require attention from a holistic practitioner.

Homeopathic treatment prescribed by a trained and experienced homeopath is always an indicated and beneficial form of treatment for these children. In one study, treatment with homeopathy proved to be more effective than using antibiotics and other drugs like Tylenol (acetaminophen) to decrease the number of ear infections over a one-year period in children with recurrent ear infections. Recurrences of ear infections were eliminated in 71 percent of the homeopathically treated cases, compared to 56 percent in the conventionally treated group (Friese et al. 1997).

I conducted a survey of children in my practice who suffered from repeated ear infections and were treated with homeopathy alone. Over 80 percent of parents who completed this survey confirmed that the frequency of ear infections improved after homeopathic treatment.

middle-ear fluid

Middle-ear infections are often accompanied by fluid production and accumulation in the middle-ear cavity. Sinus congestion and nasal congestion are also frequently accompanied by ear congestion. However, when there is fluid collection in a baby's middle ear, it tends to persist because the middle ear does not drain well in babies. The Eustachian tube is small, and its musculature does not yet function efficiently. Both of these factors tend to cause fluid to collect. A third factor is that the Eustachian tubes in babies has a more horizontal position in the skull compared to older children, whose Eustachian tubes sit more vertically, allowing gravity to help drain fluid from the middle ear. All of these factors lend themselves to fluid collection, or *middle-ear effusion*.

Fluid in the middle ear is uncomfortable and feels stuffy, leading babies to rub their ears. Older babies may have noticeable hearing loss from the fluid pressing against the eardrum, impeding its movement. This muffled hearing is temporary, and normal hearing returns when the fluid is gone. If children have difficulty hearing soft sounds, then they may have some trouble developing expressive language skills. It is important to make sure your baby is hearing words distinctly. If she has fluid in her ears, then speak a little more loudly than usual and make an extra effort to enunciate and name objects for your baby.

Studies of the persistent effects of this decreased hearing on language skills and auditory processing have conflicted. One study found that children who have persistent hearing loss from fluid in their ears have no associated language or cognitive problems by age four or six years (Feldman et al. 2002). However, other

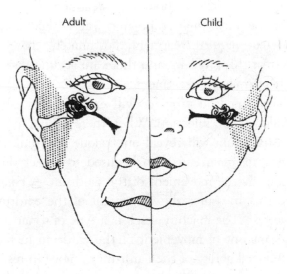

Adult   Child

Eustachian Tube

studies have found an association between fluid in the ears and consequent hearing impairment and deficits in aspects of auditory processing (visual-auditory learning, sound blending, and auditory memory) at four to nine years of age (Gravel, Wallace, and Ruben 1996). Because of these concerns, it's important to treat the fluid and make sure that children's ears are functioning normally.

Some children are especially prone to develop ear infections and fluid in their ears. Children with Down syndrome and facial-structural abnormalities (cleft lip and palate) are more likely to develop these symptoms and to require more treatment and surgical intervention.

Treatment of Middle-Ear Effusion

Fluid in the middle ear is a common occurrence during and following an ear infection. Older babies may rub their ears, and you may notice that your toddler doesn't respond to questions or hear some sounds. An exam by your pediatrician typically reveals persistent fluid in the ears and hearing loss. Normally the fluid resolves in a few weeks without any treatment. But inadequate function of the Eustachian tube may cause fluid collection to persist and may require treatment. Fortunately, there are many options to treat this problem, and there are accurate ways to evaluate the effectiveness of treatment.

Your baby's medical provider will examine her ears with an otoscope following an infection. When there is fluid in the middle ear, this visual exam will reveal an opaque eardrum. A specific test, the *tympanogram*, can then be used to detect fluid collection that impairs the movement of the eardrum. A *tympanometer* is a device that measures the movement of the eardrum with a noninvasive test. The machine itself is a type of sonar device that detects the amount of movement of the eardrum in response to sound. A reduced ability of the eardrum to move in response to a projected sound indicates a problem in the middle ear, usually due to poor function of the Eustachian tube.

Since the Eustachian tube drains through an opening into the throat, any swelling of the mucous membranes surrounding that opening may impair the ability of the middle ear to drain. Treatment targeted at decreasing that swelling is usually a part of holistic care. Other treatments can encourage the efficient function of the Eustachian tube itself and help decrease fluid production and encourage drainage.

Conventional Medical Treatment of Middle-Ear Problems

Conventional medicine has only one effective treatment for fluid in the middle ear—surgery. Under general anesthesia, ventilating tubes are placed in the eardrum, and often the adenoids or the tonsils *and* adenoids are removed. (*Adenoids* are clusters of lymph tissue behind the nose at the roof of the mouth.) A ventilating tube is a tiny, tubelike straw made of plastic or silicone inserted into the eardrum, where it then resides. During the surgical procedure, an incision is made in the eardrum and fluid is extracted from the middle ear with a suction device. Then the tube is inserted into the incision, and it remains in the eardrum. The tube equalizes the pressure in the middle ear and puts positive pressure on the fluid, resulting in increased drainage through the Eustachian tube. The ventilating tube is eventually expelled from the eardrum after a period of several months, though the tubes may stay in place for years.

During the placement of ventilating tubes, the adenoids may also be removed. The argument for removal of the adenoids rests on the theory that chronic inflammation and infection in adenoid tissue can affect the Eustachian tube and the middle ear, contributing to recurrent infections (Abdullah et al. 2006). Some studies show that adenoidectomy results in fewer subsequent ear infections (Paradise et al. 1990). Other studies show no effect on recurrences of ear infections (Hammaren-Malmi et al. 2005). And several

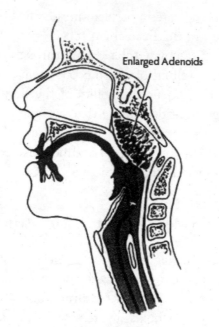

Enlarged Adenoids

other studies have shown no benefit at all from adenoid removal on fluid collection (Widemar et al. 1985; Roydhouse 1980).

Ventilating tubes fix the functional problem, and they are effective. But they do not address the underlying issues that led to the problem, which include excess mucus production, lowered resistance of the immune system, swelling of mucous membranes and lymph tissue (adenoids), and impaired or deficient function of the Eustachian tube. Once the tubes fall out, the problem tends to recur, and repeated placement of ventilating tubes is a common practice. Ventilating tubes also have side effects. These include scarring of the eardrum and an increased likelihood of infections in the middle ear. These infections are a result of the opening to the outside world that has been created, an access point for bacteria to enter the middle-ear space that is usually protected by the intact eardrum. Whether or not ventilating tubes are inserted, children need to have the underlying problem addressed or the mucus production and respiratory congestion will tend to persist.

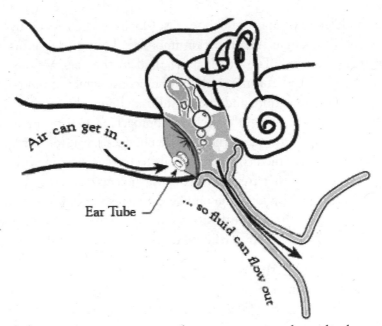

Air can get in ...

Ear Tube

... so fluid can flow out

Other treatments are used in conventional medical care, including antibiotics and decongestants. Antibiotics may sterilize the middle ear, but they do nothing for the fluid collecting there. Decongestants and antihistamines do not clear fluid from the middle ear, and they have significant adverse effects (Griffin et al. 2006).

If alternative therapies have the ability to improve Eustachian tube function, decrease mucus production, and decrease inflammation in the middle ear, nose, and throat, then those therapies may allow parents and physicians to avoid surgery for these children. That is precisely what we see with the use of holistic medical treatment of these ear problems in babies and toddlers.

Holistic Treatment of Middle-Ear Problems

Holistic care provides comprehensive treatment for the recurrent or persistent ear problems that are so common in young children. The symptoms of ear infections and fluid collection in the middle ear often begin in a baby's first year. They can persist into the toddler years and preschool ages. Once children reach five or six and Eustachian tube function improves, kids tend to grow out of these ailments. The problems of fluid in the ears with associated hearing loss, chronic swelling of mucous membranes, lowered resistance to infection, and impaired Eustachian tube function can all be addressed using a combined approach of holistic methods. Everyone can easily adopt the lifestyle changes suggested here, and you can seek out medical professionals to treat your baby with one or more of the other treatments in your holistic plan.

Don't expect fluid in the middle ear to resolve quickly. It takes at least two to three months to resolve the issues that contribute to the fluid buildup and facilitate drainage of the middle ear.

Lifestyle changes. Stop giving dairy products. The most common reason for production and stagnation of phlegm is milk products. Milk causes phlegm in many children, and other children are allergic to dairy products. This includes cheese, yogurt, and butter. Of course, allergies may contribute to ear problems and chronic congestion. In older children, environmental allergens may play a part, and at any age, food sensitivities may be a subtle contributor to these problems. Allergy testing can be helpful to assess these in children over eighteen months of age. Allergies and congestion are discussed in greater detail in chapters 7 and 8.

Chinese herbs. Fluid collection in the ears represents just one aspect of the Phlegm Dampness syndrome that plagues so many children. They often need Chinese herbal formulas as a part of a treatment program that addresses the important issue of mucus production. Your Chinese herbalist will be able to design a specific, individualized program of herbs that will help your baby overcome these problems. This may involve herbs to bolster immune function, herbs to combat the Heat and pathogenic factors that contribute to recurrent or chronic ear infections, and herbs to relieve Phlegm.

One very important formula for this purpose is Minor Bupleurum (Xiao Chai Hu Tang). Blue Poppy Pediatric Formulas makes a modified version of this formula that specifically addresses ear problems (Bupleurum & Angelica Formula). The formula addresses the digestive dysfunction that leads to Dampness and Phlegm production.

Other formulas such as Grow and Thrive by Chinese Medicine Works promote healthy digestive function and a strong immune system. Specific formulas may be needed to address the mucus production if that is a prominent factor in the child's case. There are many such formulas for your herbalist to prescribe. Other symptoms like coughing or accompanying allergies may indicate the need for a staged program of herbal treatment that heals the different layers of the problem in a case with different facets and imbalances.

Nutritional supplements. Mucus collection in the ears or sinuses signifies an inflammatory process, and an omega-3 supplement in the form of fish oil is indicated to relieve this state. Since infection is commonly a component of the middle-ear problem, a probiotic supplement will help to normalize the flora and prevent infections, especially if your baby has previously received antibiotics. Other immune-system activators will also help prevent these infections, including colostrum, whey protein, or a mushroom formula (reishi, shiitake, cordyceps). Vitamin D3 is essential for adequate immune-system function during the winter months when there is minimal sunlight (see chapter 8).

Homeopathy. Homeopathy provides a powerful tool for improving the constitutional health of babies with ear problems. It also has specific remedies for improving the function of the Eustachian tube. The most commonly indicated homeopathic remedies for middle-ear effusion (according to nineteenth-century homeopathic ear specialists and confirmed by clinical experience since then) are *Kali muriaticum* and *Mercurius dulcis* (Houghton 1875; Houghton 1885). Do not be alarmed by the suggestion of mercury in the name of the latter remedy. Homeopathic preparations of mercury have no actual molecules of mercury compounds or elemental mercury in the preparation.

Kali muriaticum (potassium chloride) is more often indicated when children have a white or greenish yellow nasal discharge, enlarged tonsils, and a stuffy sensation in the ear with hearing loss. *Mercurius dulcis* (mercury chloride), by contrast, is appropriate when the child has thickened, retracted eardrums with more scarring and a granular appearance of the tonsils as well. *Merc-dulc* shares similar symptomatology with other forms of homeopathic mercury, including diarrhea with greenish stools. A differentiating point in older children is that cold drinks ameliorate the conditions requiring *Merc-dulc*, but cold air and cold drinks aggravate the conditions requiring *Kali muriaticum*.

Kali sulphuricum is another important remedy for consideration in middle-ear effusion. Conditions that indicate *Kali-sulph* include discharges that are thin, yellow, and sticky accompanied by hearing loss from the effusion. Noises in the ears are common in older children who need *Kali-sulph*, accompanied by itching of the ears and evening pain.

Chiropractic adjustment. Classical chiropractic theory recognizes that misalignment of the spine in babies can pull on the muscles of the neck, causing tension and dysfunction of the associated organs. Proper function of the Eustachian tube depends upon balanced head and neck musculature. Correcting an imbalance in these structures allows for healthy function of the Eustachian tube, which drains fluid from the middle ear and distributes air to the middle-ear cavity. Correcting any misalignment of the spine in the neck also improves immune-system function because the first and second spinal nerves have a direct effect on immune-system responses.

The Eustachian tube resides in a bony canal of the skull and passes through the temporal and sphenoid bones. A misalignment of these bones in babies can put pressure on the Eustachian tube. Cranial adjustment and restoration of proper alignment of these bones and the cartilage of the Eustachian tube will take pressure off the tube and help restore normal function.

Chiropractic care as part of a complete holistic program for managing middle-ear problems of fluid collection and recurrent infections will work to establish both a normal function of the structures in the ear and the health of the immune system.

Prevention of Chronic Middle Ear Effusion

It starts as a cold, then your baby starts crying with an earache. Antibiotics are prescribed. A few weeks later, the pediatrician sees red eardrums again. More antibiotics. Congestion persists, and your doctor says your baby has fluid in the ears. Before you know it, she's scheduled for surgery for tubes in the ears and removal of the adenoids.

This is an all-too-common scenario. And the entire problem can be prevented with holistic pediatric care of ear infections and the accompanying congestion. Even after antibiotics have been used, these recurrences of infections can be stopped and prevented with a holistic treatment plan.

summary

The holistic solution to both acute and recurrent ear infections is to treat children with herbs and homeopathy during any acute episodes and develop a holistic medical plan for preventing recurrences and resolving chronic fluid collection in the middle ear. As we've seen, the plan can include a wide range of therapies—nutritional supplements, herbs, homeopathy, and chiropractic. If there are other accompanying problems, such as suspected allergies or a digestive imbalance, then these multiple issues will be part of an overall holistic perspective for your child's condition. A trained holistic pediatric practitioner will be able to easily manage these ear problems and usually prevent the need for surgery. Tubes may sometimes be needed if persistent fluid does not resolve. But even if surgery is necessary, the underlying issues of lowered resistance and phlegm production can be cured with a holistic healing plan.

CHAPTER 7

----

asthma and wheezing

asthma can be scary for parents. And asthma can be managed with natural, holistic methods. Armed with the information contained in this chapter and a good holistic pediatric practitioner, you can overcome your baby's respiratory symptoms and avoid the use of most conventional drugs. This chapter will define the different types of wheezing and asthma and show you how to take a proactive approach to overcome these problems using holistic pediatric methods. Asthma is often reserved as a diagnosis until babies are toddlers, but most of the information contained in this chapter can be applied equally to babies and to older toddlers and preschool children.

Not all wheezing is asthma, and not all babies with asthma have wheezing. Babies may have wheezing for a variety of reasons.

Some babies may have wheezing when they get colds. This is a response to the virus, which may be followed in later years by allergic asthma, or babies may grow out of it. Other babies with asthma may get tight, high-pitched coughs without wheezing. Usually, these children will all get a prescription for a *bronchodilator* (a drug that expands the narrowed airway) from their pediatrician. They may also get other drugs, depending on whether there is an infection and whether or not the bronchodilator completely controls their symptoms. If the symptoms continue to reappear in episodes over more than six months, then your doctor will probably diagnose asthma.

Whatever the diagnosis and the particular manifestation of recurrent wheezing and coughing in your baby, the symptoms can usually be controlled and the problem improved with a holistic management plan. In the following sections I will define the different problems associated with wheezing and help you develop a plan for long-term management.

types of wheezing and symptoms of asthma

Wheezing is an audible whistling sound that occurs during respiration. You can also hear a squeaking sound if you put your ear to your baby's chest or back or listen with a stethoscope. Usually you hear the squeaking on exhalation. Wheezing is caused by constriction of the small airways in the lungs, the *bronchi* and *bronchioles*. The size of the airway may be narrowed for several reasons. When it is, then children have difficulty breathing. Air tends to get trapped in the lungs, and children must pull to get enough air in and out. Parents will see labored breathing or gasping.

Constriction of the airway occurs for three reasons:

- Tightening of the muscles that encircle the airways. This often occurs as an allergic response, but it can occur in response to a virus or to cold or exertion.

- Swelling of the airway's mucous membrane lining. This is an inflammatory response. The swelling will narrow the airway space.

- Mucus clogging the airway. This mucous will partially block the airway, making it harder to get air through the tube.

The inflammatory process that occurs in the airway can stimulate the characteristic tight, dry cough of asthma. And the mucous that accumulates in the airway can also cause coughing in an effort to clear it.

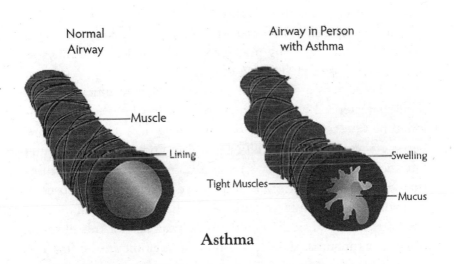

Asthma

The symptoms of asthma are coughing and wheezing. These symptoms typically occur more at night, when the body's natural levels of anti-inflammatory cortisol are at their lowest level.

Wheezing with Colds

Some babies will have wheezing in response to a respiratory viral illness, and pediatricians have different names for this phenomenon. They often avoid the term asthma, which connotes an ongoing, chronic problem. It has been called hyperactive airways, hyperreactive airways, reactive airway disease, and twitchy airways. None of these terms are very meaningful, and they may be confusing to parents. There is some evidence that suggests these episodes of wheezing with colds also have an allergic component and that wheezing in these circumstances indicates a predisposition to allergies (Rakes et al. 1999). And some experts in respiratory medicine consider these episodes of viral-induced wheezing to be an early form of childhood asthma. In one study, babies who had wheezing with a rhinovirus (the most common cause of colds) during the first year of life were three times as likely to have asthma at age six when compared to children who did not have early wheezing, and babies with wheezing in their second year were six times as likely to have asthma (Jackson et al. 2008).

Bronchiolitis is a term used to describe a viral illness in children characterized by cold symptoms that last for a few days followed by wheezing that lasts for a few more days. Symptoms may become severe, with difficulty breathing and a rapid breathing rate. Sometimes these babies require hospitalization. The viruses that cause bronchiolitis are respiratory syncytial virus, usually occurring in the winter months, and rhinovirus, usually occurring in the fall and spring months. The peak age for this illness is three to six months, though it can occur anytime in the first few years of life. Because an infant's airways are so small, the mucus produced as a result of the viral illness gets stuck in the airways and produces these sometimes-alarming symptoms. Susceptibility to allergies, genetics, a weakened immune system from birth, or a combination of these factors may also play a role in the development of asthma.

Asthma Symptoms

Here is a list of the symptoms of asthma. Your baby may have some, but probably not all of them.

---

symptoms of asthma

- Wheezing
- Rumbling sounds in the chest
- Coughing
- Shortness of breath
- Rapid breathing
- Rapid heart rate
- Labored breathing

These symptoms occur in episodes. Your baby will be fine for a time—for days, weeks, or months. Then something will trigger an asthma episode. Triggers can include an illness, exposure to something toxic in the environment, an allergic reaction to foods or something inhaled, exercise, physical or emotional stress, or a response to medications or drugs. I'll discuss these in more detail later in this chapter. Symptoms during the episode may be mild or more worrisome, depending on the individual child. Episodes may last for a few hours to several days, and the sooner you begin treatment, the more likely you are to relieve symptoms and cut short that episode.

Asthma Danger Signs

The severity of your child's asthma will dictate how vigilant you need to be about avoiding triggers and monitoring the effect of treatment during episodes. If your child tends to develop severe symptoms, then you need to know when to seek urgent medical care. Here are some danger signs.

asthma danger signs

- Retractions
- Grunting
- Little to no wheezing
- Color change (pale, ashen, blue)
- Change in mental status
- Extreme sleepiness and the inability to waken

The first signs of worsening symptoms will be air hunger and gasping for breath. This will be accompanied by *retractions*. You can see retractions when the spaces above the collar bone and between and below the ribs are sucked in as your baby tries to get a breath. This is an indication that your child is not getting enough air. You need to communicate these symptoms to your doctor or get your baby to an urgent-care facility or emergency room whenever any of these signs appear.

causes of asthma

Why do babies develop asthma? There are many predisposing factors that could be responsible, and these can interact with or complicate each other in countless different ways. Then there are many triggers that can initiate individual asthma episodes. You have the power to influence many of these through avoidance and holistic treatment methods. An understanding of causes will help lead you in the right direction toward curing your child of asthma and other allergies.

Predisposing Factors

In this section, I will go over the many possible reasons that babies develop asthma. Then, in the section on treatment, you will learn methods to improve most of these.

---

predisposing factors for asthma

- Family and genetic history
- Pregnancy history and maternal health
- Immune dysfunction
- Diet
- Environmental factors
- Drugs: Vaccines and antibiotics
- Intestinal, skin, or respiratory illness

Genetic History

If a parent or other close family member has a history of allergies, eczema, or asthma, the baby is more likely to develop these symptoms too. However, even a genetic predisposition can be overcome. Gene expression is turned on and off all the time. Improving the inner ecology of the body can create an environment where genes that cause symptoms will not express themselves.

Pregnancy History and Maternal Health

A pregnancy that is healthy, with a good diet rich in whole foods and antioxidants, will go a long way toward producing a healthy, robust baby. Supplements of probiotics and omega-3 fats from fish oil may also help prevent the development of allergies and asthma in babies (Wickens et al. 2008). Mothers who have repeated pregnancies usually become energetically deficient unless they take measures to tonify fundamental sources of energy. The energy expended in pregnancies, birthing, and breastfeeding requires replenishing to avoid deficiencies that can be passed on to babies. In Chinese terms, a deficiency of Prenatal Qi is one of the primary causes of immune-system weakness and susceptibility to external pathogens. A mother who seeks out the care of a Chinese herbalist before and during her pregnancy is more likely to have a robust and healthy baby.

Immune Dysfunction

Your baby's immune system may be hampered by a number of factors, which we examined in the chapters on digestive and skin problems (2 and 3) and which we'll review in more detail in chapter 8. Fortunately, most of these immune disorders and deficiencies can be ameliorated by holistic methods. The most common immune dysfunction arises from the leaky gut syndrome, which involves injury to the lining of the small intestine and consequent growth of pathogens there. The layer of cells that forms the intestinal barrier is damaged, allowing leakage of large protein molecules and yeast into the bloodstream. The body then produces antibodies to fight off these foreign elements. When the body later encounters these proteins from foods, the antibodies trigger allergic reactions and inflammation.

Other immune-system problems may come into play as well, including a lowered resistance to pathogens and an increased susceptibility to viral illness. The body's continued production of mucus in response to these illnesses tends to clog up the sinus passages and airways. In Chinese medical terms, another mechanism is at work. The Wei Qi, or Protective Qi of the body, may be low as a consequence of other energetic deficiencies. These imbalances will need to be corrected.

Diet: What Mom Eats

A deficient maternal diet can cause weaknesses in babies and increased susceptibility to illness. Conversely, a healthy maternal diet during pregnancy can have a significant protective effect, discouraging the development of asthma. Studies have shown that eating a whole-foods diet during pregnancy reduces the risk of asthma in children born to those mothers. The most typical dietary evaluation tool used in these studies is the Mediterranean diet score. This tool applies points for inclusion of vegetables (excluding potatoes), fruits, nuts, legumes, grains, fish, and monounsaturated fats in the diet on a daily basis. The traditional Mediterranean diet contains a high proportion of fruits, vegetables, beans, nuts, and seeds and is high in essential fatty acids, fiber, polyphenols from olive oil, and vitamins E and C. Researchers have discovered that a high Mediterranean diet score (eating a greater proportion of these foods) has a preventive effect on asthma occurrence in children.

For example, children in rural Crete have an especially low incidence of allergies and wheezing (asthma). The diet among this population is typically high in locally grown fruits and vegetables. These facts led researchers to examine whether there was an association between diet and asthma in these children. One study discovered that when mothers had a higher Mediterranean diet score during their pregnancy, their children had significantly fewer asthma symptoms at six years old compared to mothers with a lower score (Chatzi et al. 2008).

A similar study in Mexico showed that when mothers ate more fish during their pregnancy, their children had less eczema at one year of age and less asthma at age six. The amount of fish intake correlated with a protective effect against asthma. When mothers consumed fish an average of two and a half days per week during their pregnancy, their children had 37 percent less eczema at age one year and 35 percent fewer allergies at age six compared to children of mothers who ate fish once a week. The authors attribute the beneficial effect of fish to their high omega-3 fat content (Romieu et al. 2007). Because of the high pesticide and mercury content of most fish, I recommend that children get these omega-3 fats from fish-oil supplements that are free of these contaminants.

An increased intake of vitamin D3 during pregnancy is also associated with less asthma in young children. Even an increase of 100 IU of vitamin D3 daily during pregnancy decreased the risk of children acquiring asthma in one study that examined this association (Camargo et al. 2007).

Diet: What Baby Eats

One of the most important measures for preventing childhood asthma is breastfeeding. Babies who breastfeed have less asthma. Even breastfeeding for fewer than three months is correlated with a reduced risk of asthma in children. The authors of one study estimated that not breastfeeding was associated with 16 percent of asthma cases in the group of preschool children studied (Haby et al. 2001). Another study found that exclusive breastfeeding for at least four months was associated with a reduced risk of asthma (Oddy et al. 1999).

For older children, the importance of a healthy diet is underscored by several studies that have associated asthma incidence with various dietary habits. Children with healthier diets tend to have less asthma. What researchers have found can reassure and inspire all parents to pursue a healthy, whole-foods diet for their children.

One study included 690 children aged seven to eighteen years. These children were living in rural areas of Crete and were observed for dietary practices and the occurrence of allergic symptoms including asthma. The researchers discovered that children with a daily consumption of grapes, oranges, apples, and fresh tomatoes had less asthma. Eating nuts more than three times per week was also associated with less wheezing. In this study, children with a primarily Mediterranean diet had a lower incidence of nasal allergies and nighttime coughing (Chatzi et al. 2007).

The message from this study is clearly that children with allergies may benefit from eating a diet with a high proportion of fruits and vegetables, and that this type of diet may be preventive for allergies and asthma as well. Make fruits available to older children throughout the day. Pack fruits in school and camp lunches, and avoid processed foods with added sugar and corn syrup. Never use margarine. And don't forget to include nuts in children's diets as well (including walnuts, pecans, and almonds), but not until at least two years of age.

Another study found a higher incidence of asthma in preschool children who consumed higher amounts of polyunsaturated fats from vegetable oils (Haby et al. 2001), which typically contain relatively high amounts of omega-6 fatty acids. The authors of that study estimated that a diet high in polyunsaturated fats accounted for 17 percent of asthma cases in these children. Other authors have commented that the increased incidence of asthma in children found in that study could be attributed to the reduced ratio of more healthful omega-3 fats in relation to omega-6 fats (Mermer and Mercola 2002). For this reason, children who consume more fish that contains high levels of omega-3 fats also have a reduced asthma risk (Hodge et al. 1996).

A study from New Zealand looked at the other side of the food spectrum, the association between fast food and asthma in children (Wickens et al. 2005). Researchers discovered that the more fast food consumed (hamburgers and deep-fried foods), the higher the incidence of asthmatic signs and symptoms.

That study recorded the frequency of different foods consumed through a parent questionnaire, measured lung capacity in children after exercise, then correlated the two. Those researchers found that the amount of fast foods consumed corresponded to the degree of asthma as determined by the change in respiratory volume measurements before and after exercise. The correlation between asthma and foods was true for hamburgers, fried foods (fish and chips), and fizzy drinks (soda). The higher the intake of these foods, the more asthma symptoms occurred. The consumption of other foods was not associated with any outcome, either positive or negative, in relation to lung function. Those other foods included meat, fish, vegetables, fresh fruit, and fruit juice. The authors speculate that the amount of fruit consumed did not show a positive correlation with a reduction in asthma symptoms because the study was conducted in a fruit-growing area where fruit is readily and cheaply available. All of these findings were independent of other factors, including childhood obesity and socioeconomic factors.

The authors note that several other studies have seen similar associations. For example, fast food was also a risk factor for wheezing among children in Saudi Arabia, and deep-fried food consumption doubled the risk of asthma among teenagers in Taiwan. They also note that other studies have shown that children who consumed fresh fruit five to seven times a week compared with less than once a week had less wheezing, and that Australian children who ate fish high in omega-3 fats also had a reduced risk of asthma.

The proper introduction of solid foods into your baby's diet is also an important component in an allergy-protection program. Beginning foods, especially grains, at too young an age is associated with a higher risk of allergies in babies (Forsyth et al. 1993). The food guidelines outlined in my *Child Health Guide* describe the best way to begin solids. This includes delaying all grains until babies are at least twelve months old, waiting until at least ten to twelve months for dairy products in the form of yogurt and cheese, waiting until eighteen to twenty-four months for whole milk, and supplementing babies with adequate amounts of vitamins and fats as outlined in the next chapter. If babies are being fed with formula, then special attention needs to be directed at immune-system supplements.

Environmental Factors

Repeated exposure to toxins in the home can significantly contribute to the development and continuation of asthma. The most harmful of these is cigarette smoke (Dekker et al. 1991), but wood smoke from fireplaces and wood-burning stoves in the first year of life can also contribute to the development of asthma (Salam et al. 2004). Other environmental conditions in the home, including dampness, mold, and the presence of cockroaches, can contribute to the development of asthma (Krieger et al. 2000). Exposure to pesticides and herbicides is also associated with a risk of asthma in childhood. This is especially true for children continually exposed on farms, where chemicals are brought into the house on shoes and clothing (Salam et al. 2004). Maintaining a policy of no shoes in the house will prevent tracking in petrochemicals from the street and pesticides used on vegetation and crops. Farming family members can change their clothing if they have been working with pesticides. And homeowners can avoid the use of pesticides in and around the house. Other aerosolized petrochemical products should be banned as well, including commercial cleaning products and air fresheners.

Drugs: Vaccines and Antibiotics

Vaccination seems to be a risk factor for the development of asthma. I discussed the mechanisms and research surrounding the association between asthma as a side effect of vaccines in chapter 3. The theory that vaccines shift the immune system to a mode of hyperreactivity accompanied by overabundant antibody production and allergic responses is borne out by several studies that show a higher incidence of asthma in vaccinated compared to unvaccinated children. The most suggestive of these studies was a 2005 survey published in the *Journal of Allergy and Clinical*

Immunology that included 1,177 vaccinated and unvaccinated children. That survey showed that children with no family history of asthma and no antibiotics were eleven times less likely to report asthma if unvaccinated. All others in the study, those that had a family history or had taken antibiotics, were less than half as likely to develop asthma if unvaccinated (Enriquez et al. 2005).

The incidence of asthma in children has doubled since the 1970s, when the number of vaccines given to children began to multiply. In 1970, children received four different vaccines, including those for DPT and polio. Today, children receive at least eleven different vaccines in multiple doses, some of which are given at birth. As the number of different vaccines has increased, so has the incidence of asthma. No other factors correlate as well. Possibly there are more pesticides in the environment and the food supply. Perhaps the increase in pesticides in breast milk and foods given to children does play a part in the widespread immune dysfunctions we see today. Certainly a lower standard of living in urban communities contributes to the higher incidence there than in other areas. It is estimated that 15 percent of children in the United States have asthma, but a screening program of children attending school in Harlem discovered that 30 percent of children there have asthma (Nicholas et al. 2005). This high incidence could be a product of poor nutrition, pollution in this heavily populated area, and exposure to allergenic animals (dust mites and cockroaches). Air quality does not seem to be responsible for the continually increasing incidence of asthma in children, since the quality of the air and the degree of the major pollutants associated with asthma have steadily improved since the 1970s. Vaccines remain the most likely contributor to the increase in asthma in all socioeconomic strata of the population. Vaccines are given to everyone in a compulsory and systematic coverage plan that includes all children.

Many studies have shown an increased risk of asthma in children treated with antibiotics in the first year of life (Cohet et al. 2004). This association is consistent with the theory that increased exposure to bacteria and other microorganisms in the environment has a protective effect on the development of asthma (the "hygiene hypothesis"). One study that verifies this theory discovered that children raised on farms had a lower incidence of asthma compared to other children in the community. The more exposure to farm life (in hours per day) and to farm animals, the lower the risk of asthma in those children. The conclusion of that study was that increased exposure to the bacterial compounds found in stables where livestock were kept correlated with a decreased risk of asthma in children (Von Ehrenstein et al. 2000). Antibiotics will also drastically alter the delicate balance of intestinal flora, which then can cascade into intestinal inflammation and immune dysfunction and deficiency.

Intestinal, Skin, or Respiratory Illness

In this book I have already discussed many of the precursors and associated problems of asthma. These include digestive dysfunction and leaky gut syndrome, eczema, and respiratory infections with wheezing. These are multifactorial and interweaving complexes of symptoms. That is why a holistic methodology is essential to address the many factors that contribute to the development of asthma. Only in this way can we address the underlying causes of asthma, forestall the illness, and rectify the imbalances that result in this chronic and otherwise persistent problem.

Asthma Triggers

Asthma is really a disease waiting to happen. Most children tend to be symptom free between episodes, then something triggers the onset of wheezing, cough, and associated allergic symptoms. These triggers vary between children depending on the child's sensitivity and susceptibility to a wide range of factors that can include cold air, exercise, certain foods, pollens, and other types of stress. Children may also react to an allergen at some times but not at others. When your baby is already under stress from an illness or an allergic reaction, then he may start reacting to things that don't cause symptoms at other times. In this section I will review the types of triggers that can initiate the symptoms of asthma, then in the next section, on treatment, I'll discuss how to deal with these.

---

asthma triggers

- Illness
- Food reactions
- Environmental allergens (plants, animals)
- Cold air
- Exertion

Asthma tends to develop as babies get older. It is more common during the second year of life and the preschool years than in infancy. This is because it takes repeated exposure and time to develop the antibodies responsible for allergic reactions. Wheezing does occur in babies during the first year, and allergic asthma can occur in babies as young as three months, but allergies to inhaled allergens usually develop as children get older. It usually takes two seasons of exposure to become sensitized to plant pollens. When children have constant exposure to animals (cats, dogs, dust mites), they may develop these antibodies sooner, but babies are generally slow to develop the antibodies responsible for triggering asthma and other allergies to environmental allergens like plants and animals. The exception is babies with eczema, who are already producing these antibodies. About 50 percent of babies with eczema go on to develop asthma.

Illness

As I explained in the section on wheezing with colds, viruses can trigger wheezing and symptoms of asthma in babies during the first year. This may even occur every time your baby gets a cold. Doctors may not call this asthma, but regardless of the term, viruses are a potent trigger. The solution for this is to build resistance and the strength of the immune system to prevent recurrent colds.

Food Reactions

Two types of food reactions are possible. IgE reactions are immediate and can trigger an asthma episode in children who are sensitive. The most common types of foods to initiate these reactions are milk, nuts, eggs, soy, corn, and wheat. IgG reactions are a different type of immune response. They are more subtle, often delayed, and tend to result in persistent coughing and congestion.

Environmental Allergens

Environmental allergans can be separated into the plant and animal kingdoms. Most people are familiar with the role of pollens in hay fever and asthma. These reactions tend to be seasonal, depending on the sensitivity. Babies in the first year may have allergic reactions to inhaled allergens, but these types of reactions are more common in older babies and young children. Trees in the winter and early spring, grasses in the summer, and molds in the fall and winter can all trigger seasonal reactions.

Common animal allergens include dust mites, cockroaches, cats, dogs, and horses. Many children with nighttime coughing are allergic to dust mites that live in mattresses and bedding.

Allergies to cats and dogs are usually obvious to parents because of the immediate reactions that children get when petting these animals—itching eyes, sneezing, and wheezing.

Cold Air

Low temperatures can stimulate wheezing. When the mucous membranes encounter cold air, capillaries quickly become engorged with blood to warm the air. This can result in swelling of the mucous membranes and congestion. Children can also have actual allergic reactions to cold air as well, including a subsequent release of *histamine* (a natural compound that is released during allergic reactions).

Exertion

Exercise-induced asthma occurs as the breathing rate accelerates during aerobic activity. The mechanism for the asthmatic reaction is unclear, but it's probably due to the rapid airflow during exertion. As the air flows in and out, the airways become dry and cool, and mucous membranes swell in order to warm the air and hydrate the lining of the airways. This can then result in a narrowing of the airway tube and consequent wheezing.

conventional treatment of ashthma: drugs

Conventional allopathic treatment for asthma consists primarily of drug therapy. There are several types of conventional drugs that treat wheezing and asthma in babies. The most commonly used drugs are bronchodilators and steroids. The specific chemicals and preparations vary over time, and new drugs are continually developed and licensed. I will discuss the most common drugs that may have been prescribed by your baby's physician.

Bronchodilators

A bronchodilator relaxes the bands of smooth muscle that surround the airway. Smooth muscle is present in hollow organs such as the airways, blood vessels, intestines, and bladder. The smooth muscle that surrounds the tubes of the airway dilates and constricts the airway to accommodate greater needs for oxygen. During an asthmatic reaction or allergic response, these bands of smooth muscle constrict, narrowing the airway. A variety of things can make these muscles relax. Several herbs have this effect, as do various pharmaceutical agents and relaxation techniques. Unfortunately, babies who have difficulty breathing have a hard time relaxing. If you stay relaxed, it will help your baby. So take some deep breaths when your baby is in distress.

The most commonly used bronchodilator drug is albuterol, sometimes known as salbutamol. Albuterol is a short-acting drug that can be used up to every four hours to treat cough and wheezing due to *bronchoconstriction* (a tightening of the bands of muscle that encircle the airways). The medication is used in a *nebulizer*, a machine that aerosolizes the drug so that your baby can breathe it in a mist through a face mask. A *puffer*, or metered-dose inhaler, can be used to dispense the drug as well. The inhaler is sprayed into a cylindrical holding chamber that keeps the drug suspended in air so that your baby can breathe it through an attached face mask. For some babies, albuterol has a stimulating effect like caffeine that may cause increased heart rate, sleeplessness, jitteriness, and hyperactive behavior.

Another drug, levalbuterol (Xopenex), may be prescribed if albuterol produces significant side effects. Some children seem to tolerate levalbuterol better than albuterol, especially those children who are sensitive to albuterol's speedy effects. One drawback of using levalbuterol is the cost, which can be five to ten times greater than that of albuterol. However, levalbuterol purportedly has less of the excitatory effects of albuterol and less of the drug is needed, so children's sleep is not disturbed and they are less hyper.

In one study in children, albuterol did increase heart rate more than levalbuterol, but the dose of albuterol was eight times greater than levalbuterol (Milgrom et al. 2001).

If your baby has a history of wheezing, you should have one of these bronchodilators and a nebulizer or inhaler with a holding chamber at home. It may prevent a trip to the emergency room one night.

Steroids

Steroid drugs address the second mechanism that reduces the size of the airway, inflammation. The effect of steroids is to decrease the swelling of mucous membranes that line the airway. Because steroids have an anti-inflammatory effect, they will also decrease mucus production. If your baby has a history of wheezing, your pediatrician or allergist will prescribe an inhaled steroid drug to use on a daily basis whenever your baby has a cold or cough. The physician may also prescribe a steroid for everyday use as a means to prevent asthma symptoms. Inhaled steroids work directly on the lungs, reducing the risk of immune-system suppression that occurs with systemic steroid use. Systemic steroids given orally are usually reserved for severe asthma episodes that are not controlled by other drugs. And because of the potentially harmful effects of steroid drugs, they are only used for a short period of time to bring symptoms under control.

However, even inhaled steroids can have significant side effects. The most worrisome side effect is the suppression or reduction of your baby's hormones as a result of the drug, including growth hormone, resulting in growth delays in children who use inhaled steroids. An analysis of five studies that examined the association of inhaled steroids and growth revealed that moderate doses of an inhaled steroid, beclomethasone, in children with mild to moderate asthma caused a significant decrease in growth of 0.6 inch per year (Sharek and Bergman 2000). Other studies have shown a growth delay in the first year of steroid use, but attainment of normal stature when children were observed over many years (Childhood Asthma Management Research Group 2000).

Most holistic practitioners would agree that steroid use will interfere with other natural interventions to improve children's health. This is because of the immune-suppressing effects of steroid drugs. For these reasons, steroid drugs are best avoided whenever possible. They are seldom needed in babies receiving holistic care because other forms of treatment will serve the same function of decreasing and preventing inflammation of the airways without causing any side effects.

Now let's move on to consider the holistic approach to treating and preventing asthma symptoms.

holistic management of asthma

The holistic approach to asthma treatment requires multiple steps and multiple disciplines. Treatment involves three components:

■ **Monitor symptoms and treat acute episodes.** It is important that you understand and can recognize your baby's asthma symptoms. That way, you can monitor how he's doing and will know when he's running into trouble. You can begin treatment at home at the onset of symptoms or consult with your child's medical provider. Treatment for asthmatic episodes (coughing and wheezing) usually takes the form of herbs, acupuncture, chiropractic, and homeopathic medicines to alleviate and control symptoms. These methods may be combined with conventional drugs for wheezing, if needed.

■ **Manage allergens.** Identify, reduce, modify, or eliminate contributing dietary and environmental factors. This preventive approach will reduce exposure to asthma triggers and thereby prevent allergic reactions, wheezing episodes, and coughing.

■ **Balance and strengthen immune function.** The most important and most successful part of the management plan involves deep-acting, constitutional treatment and nutritional support that correct the underlying imbalance that causes asthma in your child. This will result in a stronger and less reactive immune system. Remember that the body has its own system of anti-inflammatory processes and chemicals that can prevent allergic reactions. When these are supported through treatment, your child will experience fewer symptoms. This component of treatment will involve nutritional supplements and herbal medicines. A constitutional homeopathic medicine prescribed by a qualified homeopathic practitioner can be invaluable to stimulate healing.

Parent participation in the holistic treatment plan involves identifying the symptoms of asthma, determining how severe an episode is, beginning appropriate methods in early stages of symptoms to bring them under control, and communicating with your holistic doctor to continue improving your baby's health. You will quickly become expert in using the interventions that work best for your baby. The preventive measures include daily supplements to give your baby on an ongoing basis as well. Parents can see impressive results with this integrated treatment system, with significantly less severe and less frequent episodes of wheezing and a more resilient immune system.

Monitor and Treat Symptoms

If your baby is coughing or wheezing, it's important to be aware of the severity of his symptoms. The signs of worsening symptoms are fast respiration, gasping for air, and pulling for breath with retractions. Look for retractions in the areas above the collarbone and between the ribs. If those areas are being sucked in when your baby tries to pull for air, then he is in trouble and you need to seek assistance from a medical provider to get his airways open.

It makes sense to begin holistic acute treatment as soon as possible during a cold or the first onset of coughing, especially if you know your baby tends to develop wheezing. Then monitor your child's response to treatment. Improvement in symptoms should include a decrease in the frequency and severity of coughing, less difficulty breathing, and gradual reduction in congestion.

If your baby has a cough and then subsequently develops a fever, that may be a sign of a worsening infection. In that situation, consult with your child's medical provider.

Manage Allergens

The second step in your asthma-management program is to learn what factors trigger allergic responses and limit your baby's exposure to them when possible. Managing allergens in your baby's life is an important aspect of reducing his asthma symptoms.

Allergy Tests

Should your baby or small child be tested for sensitivity to allergens? First let's consider the tests, then we'll discuss the factors that may make you choose to get some allergen testing done.

There are three types of allergy testing. The first is a blood test for IgE antibodies to foods and environmental allergens known as the *RAST test* (radioallergosorbent test). This requires a blood draw from a vein. You can apply some numbing cream obtained from a pharmacy to the crook of the elbow prior to the test to make the procedure painless. The second type of test is a patch test done by an allergist. Individual allergens are applied to scratches on the skin, and the reactions to each are observed. This is also a test for IgE-type allergic reactions. These IgE reactions occur immediately after exposure to the offending allergens. The third type of test looks for food sensitivities as opposed to immediate allergic reactions. These sensitivities can be evaluated with a blood test for IgG antibodies to foods or a blood test for white blood cell reactions to foods. Both of these tests can be done with a finger-stick blood test (US BioTek and ALCAT labs). These reactions may occur many hours after exposure to foods through breast milk or from solids. The foods can cause delayed reactions that indicate a sensitivity rather than an actual immediate allergic reaction (the IgE reaction). So this third test is looking for a different type of food sensitivity that may shed some additional light on the hidden triggers of recurrent symptoms.

Foods. For infants who have allergic-type symptoms such as eczema or wheezing, and even in babies with chronic congestion, allergy testing may give you some valuable information about foods that could be causing reactions. These foods may be contained in breast milk from mom's diet or from cow's-milk proteins in formula. Testing mothers for IgG or blood cell reactions to foods can also be useful because mothers can pass on the antibodies that cause reactions in babies. Once children are eating a wide range of foods and as babies get older, they can develop their own antibodies to foods, and IgE as well as IgG blood tests for your child could help pinpoint individual foods that contribute to symptoms. Be aware that children may react at some times to a food, but not at other times. If they are already in a reactive mode to one allergen, then they may tend to react more than they usually would to other allergens. Or you may know for sure that your baby reacts to a food because he develops symptoms whenever he gets a taste of an egg or dairy product, but nonetheless the different types of allergy tests for those foods is negative. The bottom line is that food-allergy testing can give you information and lead you in certain directions to make you cautious about certain foods, but ultimately it is your observations of your baby's reactions that will provide you with real answers. Trust your experience. To complicate issues even more, babies do grow out of food allergies and repeat testing may give you different results. The interpretation of food-allergy testing can be tricky, and an ongoing dialogue with your baby's health care provider can be invaluable.

Once you know that your baby has antibodies to particular foods, you still need to discern whether he actually reacts to those foods. You don't need to avoid a food if it's not causing symptoms. Sometimes this will be difficult to decide. For example, if your baby is chronically congested and he has a strong rating on an IgG panel for milk, it may not be obvious that milk is causing symptoms. Part of the treatment plan for your baby might include the avoidance of milk and other foods on the list with positive scores. You and your baby may need to continue avoiding these foods for several weeks or up to two or three months. For breast-fed babies, this will mean elimination of those foods from mom's diet as well. Then, when your baby's symptoms are improved as a result of the food elimination and the other treatment measures you have taken, reintroduce the foods one at a time and try to see if they are causing significant symptoms. I say "try" because results of this experiment may not be obvious. These types of symptoms tend to come and go. If your baby gets frequent colds, then congestion may occur that is unrelated to the suspect food. Many other stresses can cause recurrences of symptoms as well, so the factors responsible for symptoms may be additive or overlapping. This can be a frustrating experience. Of course, by this time your baby may have a stronger, more resilient immune system with less reactivity as a result of holistic treatment, and symptoms may not recur even if he is sensitive or allergic to specific foods.

If an IgE test shows a high score for a food, that makes it very suspect as a cause of symptoms. And some allergic reactions can be life threatening. If you know that your baby has a severe allergy to peanuts, for example, you will need to diligently avoid any exposure to this food. Your doctor will want you to carry epinephrine with you wherever you go in case of an accidental exposure.

Food-allergy testing can lead you to the avoidance of problematic foods, especially in the early stages of holistic treatment. Remember, however, that the goal of holistic care of allergies and asthma is to make children more resistant and resilient. Holistic care should result in an immune system that is not so reactive to foreign proteins, mucous membranes that are less easily inflamed, and a greater ability to calm inflammation without developing disruptive symptoms. Children are likely to become less reactive to foods and more able to tolerate them in their diets as treatment progresses.

Animals. If there are pets in the house, you will want to know if your wheezy baby is allergic to them. An IgE blood test would help identify the culprit. Then you can decide whether to find Kitty a new home or make her an outdoor cat. Similarly, if you know that your child is allergic to dust mites, you can take measures to limit exposure to them around the house. Some other inhaled allergens are difficult or impossible to avoid. Knowing that a child is allergic to grasses or trees is not going to help you much. You probably already know that your baby is allergic to grasses if he gets itchy eyes and becomes wheezy when outdoors during the summer. Testing for environmental allergens is not going to help guide you to a particular treatment, and your baby can't avoid breathing the air, so this information is not very useful except possibly to confirm what you already suspect. If you suspect that your baby has seasonal allergic reactions to plants, then run a HEPA air filter in the bedroom around the clock. This will clear the air of pollens and mold spores that might be causing allergic reactions.

Dust-mite allergies are common in children, and an IgE blood test for dust mites will reveal antibodies that presumably indicate an allergy to these microscopic creatures. However, allergy tests are not always accurate, and a negative test result does not mean that the mites do not affect your baby. Dust mites survive on shed human skin cells. So mattresses and bedding are perfect places for them to congregate and multiply. They like moisture, and they cannot survive in an atmosphere with a level of humidity less than 50 percent.

Babies who have nighttime coughing are often allergic to dust mites. Though it's impossible to get rid of the mites entirely, there are steps you can take to limit your baby's exposure. If your baby is congested and coughs at night, get proactive. Here are six steps you can take toward dust-mite prevention:

Limiting Dust-Mite Exposure

- **Cover mattress and pillows.** Purchase mattress and pillow covers from a store or website providing products for allergy sufferers. These covers are actually bags with zippers that enclose the mattress or pillow. The fabric allows air to get through, but traps the dust mites in the mattress and pillow so that your baby has no more exposure to them.

- **Wash bedding.** Wash bed coverings in hot water and dry them in the clothes dryer. This will destroy all the dust mites.

- **Treat carpets.** Purchase a carpet spray or powder that kills dust mites if the room your baby sleeps in has carpeting. These products are nontoxic to humans and household pets, but they kill the mites on contact.

- **Limit stuffed toys.** Remove stuffed animals from your baby's bed. These can harbor dust mites. Or, you can pick a favorite stuffed animal and wash it frequently in hot water.

- **Vacuum.** Vacuum the floors and mattresses often to keep dust-mite populations low.

- **Dehumidify.** Run a dehumidifier in the bedroom. Both dust mites and molds thrive in humid environments.

Balance and Strengthen Immune Function

Now we proceed to a crucial aspect of the holistic treatment of your baby's asthma. There are numerous options available to balance and regulate the immune system, to strengthen his constitution, and to support him nutritionally, all of which will help prevent and lessen the severity of his symptoms.

Chinese Medicine

Chinese medicine offers exceptionally successful treatments for asthma. In the context of this ancient science, the primary reason that babies have asthma is a deficiency of Prenatal Qi or Primordial Qi (Yuan Qi), the energetic life force transmitted from the mother to her baby. Many factors account for this deficiency. Mothers are often worn down from pregnancy, nursing, and taking care of children. This drain on the system prevents babies from being nurtured adequately during pregnancy, and the result is a diminished immune system. Chinese herbs have the ability to replenish and build Qi. If your baby takes these herbs, then he will become stronger.

Weak Prenatal Qi depletes the storehouse of energy available to other body systems, resulting in deficient Wei Qi (the protective shield that dispels external pathogens) and a lack of nourishment for production of Lung Qi. When the lungs are weak, then there will be a lack of resilience and your baby will have more difficulty with respiratory function. This is the usual source of asthma in babies—deficient Prenatal Qi resulting in deficient Lung Qi. The body also produces Qi from digestion and respiration, but if Lung Qi is weak then it cannot produce the Postnatal Qi that replenishes energy used by the body. Thus, the cycle of weakness persists. When antibiotics, steroids, and vaccines join this mix, the production of Qi is further depressed because of injury to the digestive and immune systems. If the digestive system cannot absorb nutrients well, then it will not be nourishing the lungs adequately. In

Chinese medicine, it is the Spleen (digestive system) that directly nourishes the Lung system. Therefore, the treatment of asthma and weakness of the Lung system in babies requires herbs that build Postnatal Qi, Lung Qi, and Spleen Qi.

Acupuncture

The stimulation of acupuncture points along the energetic meridians of the skin is an excellent treatment for asthma in children. Acupuncture points in babies can be stimulated in many ways: with finger pressure or massage, blunt tools, magnets, lasers, or needle insertion. Parents can learn techniques to stimulate acupuncture points, and most acupuncturists can teach parents how to use these techniques at home to treat cough, congestion, fever, and wheezing.

The treatment principles for acupuncture include tonification (strengthening treatment) of Lung, Kidney, and Spleen points, channels, and microchannels. There are also points for the relief of symptoms on the back, the chest, and the arms and hands. Here are some of the most important points:

- Lung 1, 5, 6, and 7 on the arm for cough and congestion

- Dingchuan and Bladder 13 on the back for asthma

- Stomach 40 and Large Intestine 4 for Phlegm and Dampness

- The general tonification points Stomach 36, Spleen 6, and Kidney 3

- Other points for acute episodes with illnesses (invasion of Wind Cold)

These points are well-known to all acupuncturists from classical texts. Acupuncture treatment may include special points for asthma and cough, as well as an individualized plan for your baby's constitution.

Acupressure and Massage

Parents will find that massaging specific points on their child's body during asthmatic episodes will help relieve cough, induce relaxation, and decrease wheezing. The techniques fall into two categories: pressing on acupuncture points and massage of acupuncture channels. Both techniques are simple, straightforward, and require no formal training.

There are six important acupressure points for the relief of asthma symptoms. With your child lying down, apply finger pressure to the points on both sides of the body simultaneously, if possible. Gently press and vibrate your finger or thumb on the point. Hold for about a minute; or you can hold for ten seconds, release for ten seconds, and repeat ten times. The points may be tender. Apply pressure without causing pain. Since your fingers are relatively big compared to the areas on your baby's body, if you are in about the right place you will be hitting the acupuncture point.

Here are useful acupressure points for you to try with your baby:

- **Lung 1.** Located on either side of the chest in the soft space just under the area where the collarbone joins the shoulder, this point opens blocked energy in the lungs.

- **Conception Vessel 17.** Located in the center of the chest at the level of the nipples, this point clears the lungs and disperses congestion.

- **Pericardium 6.** Located in the center of the palmar surface of the forearm (with the hand facing up), one-half inch above the crease of the wrist, this point opens the chest.

- **Ding chuan.** This is a specific point to relieve asthma. It is located on the back, just below and to the outside of the most prominent vertebra at the base of the neck.

- **Liver 3.** Located on the top of the foot in the space one-half inch up from the junction of the first and second toes, this is a calming point that brings energy down out of the chest.

- **Stomach 40.** Located one-half inch on the outside of the shinbone at a level half the distance between the prominent bones at the knee and ankle, this point relieves congestion.

Another useful acupressure technique is the more general tui na pediatric massage, a soothing and effective treatment for symptom relief in infants and children. It involves repetitive massage for thirty seconds at a time repeated two to three times per day. For massage of the limbs, do one side and then the other. Young children respond especially well to tui na.

Here are some suggested tui na massage techniques for asthma:

- **Ring finger.** Rub the palmar surface of the ring finger in a straight line from the second knuckle to the fingertip. Rub in one direction only, from knuckle to fingertip, on each hand.

- **Chest.** With thumbs together at the midpoint of the chest between the nipples (Conception Vessel 17) and hands wrapped around the chest, push the thumbs out toward the nipples. This is a different procedure than the pressure point above, as it is a massage stroke rather than simple pressure.

- **Back.** With thumbs on the inside border of the shoulder blades and hands wrapped around the back, push apart the curves of the shoulder blades with thumbs moving in one direction from above to below.

- **Forearm.** Use this one only if the child does not have a fever. Rub along the lateral edge (thumb side) of the long bone of the forearm (the *radius*) in one direction from the wrist to the elbow.

Chinese Herbs

There are two categories of Chinese herbal formulas that address asthma symptoms: those for acute episodes and those for long-term prevention and curative treatment.

A specific Chinese herbal formula has been created for treating children's acute asthma episodes. This formula, Open Air (CMW), is a variation of the formula Perilla Seed Decoction (Su Zi Jian Qi Tang). The primary ingredient is perilla seed, which has the function of dispersing and descending congested Lung Qi. Perilla has been studied in clinical trials and found to improve lung function tests in patients with asthma and inhibit the production of *leukotrienes*, an inflammatory chemical similar to histamine that stimulates asthmatic reactions (Okamoto et al. 2001). Many parents have found that Open Air can replace albuterol as a first-line medicine for wheezing and cough associated with bronchoconstriction. This is not a medicine for children with fevers or bronchitis.

A second pediatric medicine, Lung Qi Jr. (Blue Poppy), is also designed to treat wheezing and cough. This formula clears Heat, transforms Phlegm, and fortifies Qi.

Issues surrounding the use of Chinese herbal formulas to alleviate chronic symptoms, to improve immune function, and to treat constitutional imbalances in children with asthma become significantly complicated. Usually the Lungs need to be strengthened, but other organ networks require attention as well. A trained herbalist will work with the unique set of symptoms, dynamics, and characteristics of your baby to develop the correct formulas for restoring health and balance to the body. Even with a specific condition like asthma, there are many dynamics that must be considered when prescribing constitutional herbal medicines. Often these babies need replenishing of their Qi, especially if they were born with a deficiency of Prenatal Qi. Then the other dynamics will need attention as well, including strengthening digestive function (Spleen Qi), relieving Dampness, or calming the inflammation of allergic reactions (Heart Fire), for example. Then, treating the interrelationship of these energetic organ systems complicates things further. These types of theoretical underpinnings will guide the treatment principles of herbal prescribing for children with asthma.

Homeopathy

Classical homeopathy offers tremendous possibilities for children of all ages with asthma symptoms. Classical prescribing requires using one homeopathic medicine at a time and observing its effects. There are two types of homeopathic medicines for asthma, those used on an acute level to relieve symptoms during asthmatic episodes, and constitutional or deep-acting medicines that stimulate a profound healing reaction. Constitutional prescribing should be managed by a trained homeopathic practitioner, but parents can easily learn to use acute medicines. You will quickly discover the medicines that work best for your child.

Homeopathic medicines can be combined with other forms of treatment, including herbal formulas and conventional drugs when these are needed.

Acute Treatment

Asthmatic symptoms in children are characterized by either wheezing and tight breathing or coughing. Often, both occur at the same time. Homeopathic medicines can be used as often as every hour during an acute episode of cough and wheezing. The frequency of repetition will depend on the severity of symptoms, with more frequent dosing for more severe and worrisome symptoms. Choose the medicine that fits your child's symptoms most accurately during an acute episode.

Lobelia. This is the first medicine to think of when your child has short, dry coughs with wheezing. Shortness of breath is brought on by exposure to cold air and any exertion. The chest is tight and constricted.

Ipecacuanha. This corresponds to more childhood asthma symptoms than any other medicine. It can be used for racking, rattling coughs with rumbling in the chest and wheezing. It's also indicated for coughing with every breath accompanied by nausea, gagging, or vomiting. Attacks occur in warm or damp weather, and symptoms are better in the open air. Mucus collects in the throat or chest, causing a loose, gagging cough. Loud bubbling noises from the congestion can be heard in the chest on breathing.

Cuprum metallicum. This remedy is used for spasmodic coughing and spasmodic vomiting. Children who benefit from this remedy feel a painful constriction of the chest and their cough is better from drinking cold water and becomes worse in hot weather.

Sambucus. Your child will benefit from *Sambucus* when he suffers sudden, suffocative, gasping spells of asthma that resemble croup in their intensity. The child awakens nearly suffocated, gasping for air until the attack passes. He lies down afterward only to awaken again with the same symptoms. *Sambucus* fits these sudden, dramatic attacks that usually occur at night and include a hollow, dry cough that becomes worse when lying down or in cold air.

Constitutional Care

Caring for your baby's constitutional issues with a homeopathic practitioner can provide a very significant boost to healing within a holistic, integrative treatment plan that also includes herbs and nutritional supplements. Often a single dose of the correct homeopathic constitutional medicine will stimulate a healing reaction that persists for months. As part of an overall healing program, this addition to the treatment regimen can be invaluable for children with asthma. Since these symptoms are episodic and intermittent, any form of treatment that can generate a significant and permanent change for the better will contribute to a cure. Homeopathy, along with Chinese medicine, has the ability to change the fundamental energetic state of the child and move the system in the direction of cure. This is especially important in a problem as complex as asthma, where multiple factors contribute to the imbalance. Homeopathy has the ability to change and improve this imbalance at a profound level.

Nutritional Supplements

Asthma is a complex condition with many contributing and predisposing influences that have led to the development of symptoms. When prescribing a nutritional supplement plan for an individual child, these complex and overlapping factors need to be considered. The field of functional medicine has developed a model for assessing these factors and discovering the nutrients and nutritional support that will best benefit your child. I'll discuss this method more thoroughly in chapter 8. Here I will review the most common supplements that will benefit any child with asthma.

The age of a child will determine what nutrients are important to supplement. A solely breastfed baby will need different forms of supplements than a baby who is eating solids, and a toddler may need other supplements in different forms than smaller babies. Asthma is a syndrome that tends to develop when babies are a little older. And remember that the order of symptom expression in these children is often eczema as an infant developing into asthma as an older baby or toddler. The symptoms move from a more superficial level to a deeper level. This symptom expression may call for different forms of nutritional support at different times.

---

nutritional supplements for asthma

- Omega-3 fats from fish oil
- Vitamin D3 (cholecalciferol)
- Probiotics and prebiotics
- Vitamin A

Omega-3 Fats

All babies need omega-3 fats from fish oil. DHA from fish oil is necessary for brain and nerve development. EPA from fish oil has an anti-inflammatory effect. All children with allergies, asthma, or digestive inflammation associated with these problems will benefit from fish oil supplementation. Krill oil is a suitable substitute for fish oil, and krill oil has these fats in a more easily absorbed form, but krill is not a palatable form for babies. If mothers take fish oil or krill oil, then solely breastfed babies will get these fats from their mother's milk. Formula-fed babies and all babies who are eating solids can take a liquid fish-oil supplement.

Vitamin D3

All babies need to have an adequate supply of vitamin D3. Babies can get this from sun exposure during the summer, but at other times of year a vitamin D3 supplement will supply this valuable nutrient for adequate immune-system function. Even breastfed infants will benefit from vitamin D3 supplementation. Certainly any baby with recurrent illnesses or allergies needs additional vitamin D3 at all times of year other than summer. The daily dosage is 1,000 IU of vitamin D3 for babies and 2,000 IU for toddlers and older children.

Probiotics and Prebiotics

Probiotics and prebiotics are an important part of a supplement program for any baby who has been exposed to antibiotics or who tends to get respiratory or yeast infections. Stool tests for yeast and for intestinal bacteria can give a picture of the health of the digestive tract in babies and may also indicate the need for supplementation with probiotics. When allergies and asthma are associated with digestive problems, a history of reflux, or suspicions of leaky gut syndrome, then probiotics are an appropriate supplement for babies of any age. Prebiotics are nutrients that promote the growth of healthy intestinal bacteria. They are found in fruits, legumes, and whole grains, but they can be taken as supplements in powder form by babies in the form of certain sugar compounds (oligosaccharides and arabinogalactans).

The particular strains of intestinal bacteria needed by babies will differ with age and symptom expression. Generally, solely breastfed babies need *Bifidobacterium* species, and babies given any formula and older babies who have started solids need a combination of *Lactobacillus* and *Bifidobacterium*. Other strains may be needed as well, including *L. rhamnosus* and *L. reuteri* and the yeast *Saccharomyces boulardii* if there are suspicions of accompanying yeast overgrowth.

Vitamin A

Vitamin A is essential for immune-system function, including production of the blood cells that fight infections and production of antibodies, and for maintenance of healthy mucous membranes. Breast milk contains vitamin A and many other nutrients needed by babies, usually in adequate amounts for your developing infant. If you are breastfeeding, be sure that you are eating plenty of fresh fruits and vegetables, eggs, butter, and whole-milk dairy products (unless you or your baby are sensitive to dairy). Orange fruits and vegetables contain beta-carotene, which you and your baby will convert to vitamin A. Vitamin A itself is found in animal products (300 IU in an egg, 250 IU per cup of whole milk or whole-milk yogurt, and 350 IU per tablespoon of butter). After your baby is eating solids, a significant proportion of his diet should contain foods that are good sources of beta-carotene, including carrots, sweet potatoes, pumpkin, mangoes, and broccoli. Supplementation with vitamin A may interfere with vitamin D3 in the body, so it's best to rely on diet for your baby's vitamin A requirements. And remember that baby food in jars may contain significantly less vitamin content compared to freshly prepared homemade foods.

Digestive Support

Your baby needs a healthy digestive tract since most immune-system functions begin in the gut. All of the issues and suggestions in the following chapter regarding a healthy digestive system will apply to babies with asthma and wheezing. Intestinal *dysbiosis* (imbalance of intestinal bacteria) and leaky gut syndrome are very common findings in children with asthma. Correcting these digestive problems will provide the immune-system foundation that will prevent and help to solve recurrences of asthma.

prevention of asthma

We have discussed many ways that you can prevent asthma symptoms in your child, including avoidance of asthma triggers, preventive nutritional supplements, and treating the underlying constitutional weaknesses that predispose children to asthma. If your child has eczema, then applying the principles discussed in chapter 3 may even prevent the onset of asthma symptoms. And even before your baby is born, you may be able to prevent the development of allergies in your baby by taking probiotics and fish oil supplements during pregnancy.

older kids with asthma

As your baby gets older, there are many additional nutritional supplements that can help immune-system and lung function.

During the preschool years, children can begin supplementing nutrients that they no longer get from breast milk. Toddlers and preschoolers often develop food preferences that are limited, with less healthy choices than you might desire for them. Kids at this age usually like fruit, but many will decline vegetables and prefer starchy carbohydrates with low nutritional value. A supplement program that focuses on asthma and immune function can be invaluable. In addition to the supplements I discussed for babies, the antioxidant vitamins C and E will enhance immune-system function and prevent inflammation. Magnesium is a natural bronchodilator, and it also helps in stabilizing *mast cells* and preventing their release of histamine. Mast cells are present in the skin and mucous membranes, where they react with antigens and initiate allergic reactions. Magnesium and calcium come together in liquid or chewable forms because of their synergistic relationship. A calcium supplement is advisable for any child who has milk sensitivities and is therefore limiting dairy intake.

Several formulas of herbs and nutritional supplements have a beneficial effect on allergies and asthma. These formulas may contain quercetin, bromelain, stinging nettle, vitamin C, and N-acetylcysteine, all of which have antihistamine and anti-inflammatory effects in the treatment of allergies. Ortho Molecular Products makes an excellent chewable formula, D-Hist Jr., that contains this combination. Bromelain is an enzyme extracted from pineapple with anti-inflammatory effects. Quercetin is a chemical found in apple skins with antihistamine effects. Stinging nettle is a plant with antihistamine and antileukotriene effects. Histamine and leukotrienes both have a role in stimulating the inflammatory symptoms of asthma.

■ Case Report ■
Asthma

I first saw the little girl I'll call Lydia at twelve months of age. She had a history of reflux as an infant with pain on lying down. Her parents had to use a bouncer to keep her asleep with the constant motion. Lydia's digestive problems improved, but then, after six months of age, whenever she caught a cold she would have wheezing. After these colds, the resulting cough would linger, and at those times it would often trigger vomiting. Lydia's parents always used albuterol by nebulizer during these episodes.

Lydia also had some troublesome behavior problems. She was constantly squirmy and restless. It was very difficult to get her to sit in her car seat. She was never gentle. And she terrorized the family, hitting and screaming when she would get mad. She had some nervous habits, the most noticeable of which was hair pulling. She would pull and twist her own hair until it fell out.

Her treatment began with two Chinese herbal formulas, Grow and Thrive combined with Deep Breath (CMW). A supplement program included cod liver oil, chewable colostrum, a probiotic, instructions to stop dairy, and the Chinese herbal formula Open Air to use as needed for recurrences of wheezing.

One month into treatment, Lydia was much better, more relaxed, and taking better naps. Then she had a regression to her previous wild, restless behaviors, and she was given a constitutional homeopathic medicine, *Tarentula*, in a single dose. All of her symptoms dramatically improved.

Interestingly, five months after beginning treatment she developed an eczema rash on her back and hand. This was interpreted as symptoms working their way out to the surface, a common progression with homeopathic treatment. During this time she had no recurrences of her wheezing episodes.

Two months later she had a return of the screaming, squirmy, hair-pulling behaviors and the *Tarentula* was repeated. After that, Lydia needed a repeat dose of the homeopathic medicine about every six months for a return of either wheezing or her behavioral symptoms. By the time she was three years old, she was free of symptoms and doing extremely well, with no return of her asthma.

summary

Asthma is a complex condition with many symptoms and manifestations. It can begin in the first year of life with colds that cause wheezing, then progress to asthma episodes and allergic reactions. Eczema and asthma are closely related, and babies with eczema frequently develop asthma in a natural progression.

The holistic treatment of asthma will first identify causative and aggravating influences such as allergens, then balance and strengthen the immune system using a variety of methods. During the course of long-term treatment it is also important to manage the acute symptoms of asthma (wheezing and cough) with short-acting medicines that will provide relief during asthma episodes, controlling symptoms so that they do not worsen or become dangerous.

The goals of a holistic program for asthma include improvement in overall health and quality of life, lessening of the severity and frequency of asthma episodes, confidence in the ability to manage symptoms when they occur, and a gradual progression to cure—the complete elimination of asthmatic episodes. Only through a holistic program can there be hope and the expectation for overall improvement in health. Asthma is a chronic illness, but holistic medicine provides the tools and the perspective to return your baby to a state of vital resilience and robust health.

CHAPTER 8

----

the immune system:
putting it all together

Your baby is born with an immature immune system. Many systems in the body are not fully developed at birth, and the first few months of life require maturation of the nervous system, the digestive tract, and the immune system. All of this must take place at the same time that your baby is eating, digesting, and depending on the digestive system for survival. All of this development is a big job. Fortunately, babies are very good at growing and developing all the systems that they need as long as they are not hindered in this process. Provide babies with the right prenatal environment, feed them the right food, avoid toxic assaults, and everything usually goes well. However, many babies face various stresses that can undermine the normal, healthy development of the immune system.

immune-system challenges

The conventional treatment of infants with vaccines, antibiotics, and other suppressive medications often results in a depressed and unbalanced immune system. Some children are born with an inherited weakness of their immune system because of their mother's depletion or a genetic susceptibility to allergic conditions. The physical stresses of toxic chemicals can easily tip these children into a mode of reactivity, inflammation, and recurrent illness. Vaccines especially have been investigated as a causative factor in the immune-system disorders of babies that occur so commonly— recurrent infections and allergies (see chapter 3). Just at the time when immune mechanisms are developing and delicate in young babies, they are subjected to the assault of vaccines and the chemicals they contain. If babies begin getting infections as a result, they are given antibiotics that destroy the body's health-promoting bacteria along with any pathogens. Thus, the antibiotics add insult to injury and further undermine digestive function and the immune system.

In this chapter, we'll discuss the mechanisms of immune-system function and disorder, the nature of immune-system imbalance, and a method using specific measures to correct this situation and rebalance immune function. These measures include dietary interventions, nutritional supplements, and appropriate constitutional treatment by a holistic pediatric health care provider.

Before proceeding with the many options for treatment of immune dysfunction, the simple measures for prevention and dietary support of the immune system warrant mentioning. Breastfeeding establishes the ideal foundation for healthy immune function, but obviously even breastfed babies can get into immune-system trouble. Once babies begin to eat solids, using organic foods and preparing your baby's food from fresh sources at home will provide the most nutrients. Organic foods have more vitamins and antioxidants than foods grown with pesticides and fertilizers (Asami et al. 2003). And the processing and canning of foods to put them in convenient jars destroys many of their valuable nutritional components. A fresh whole-foods diet for mothers and babies sets the stage for a rich environment of vitamins, minerals, healthy fats, antioxidants, and phytonutrients that can support the healthiest immune system.

acquiring immunity

At birth, babies have a naïve immune system. They have never been exposed to pathogens in the environment or antigens through their digestive system (*antigens* are agents foreign to the body that produce an immune response). A baby gains immunity to infectious agents (viruses and bacteria) from the antibodies she receives from her mother's bloodstream. And these antibodies are short-lived. Your baby must also acquire her own immunity, a task she has never previously accomplished. Despite the presence of these maternal antibodies, the immaturity of your infant's immune system leaves her susceptible to viral and bacterial attack. Fortunately, colostrum and breast milk contain antimicrobial factors that provide protection from pathogens.

The primary protective substance in breast milk is *secretory IgA*, a form of the IgA antibody that prevents attachment and invasion of pathogens in the intestine of babies (Brandtzaeg 1998). In addition, many other components in breast milk have antimicrobial activity. For example, oligosaccharides (specific protective sugar compounds) are the third most abundant constituent of breast milk. Those oligosaccharides inhibit pathogen interactions with your baby's mucosal tissues and protect against infection. Other constituents interfere with pathogens binding to cells (Kelly and Coutts 2000). Even more importantly, breast milk actually edu-

167

cates the immune system of babies by giving coded instructions to form immune complexes and promotes the maturation of the intestinal lining, the most important organ for immune function. These attributes of breast milk show that breastfeeding stimulates and augments the function of the immune system that produces inflammation in the fight against pathogens. The body needs to fight off foreign invaders with inflammatory responses, but too much inflammation can result in persistent mucus production and digestive upsets. Amazingly, breast milk also has an immunosuppressive effect, preventing reactivity and too much inflammation. A substance in breast milk called lactoferrin especially has an anti-inflammatory effect, preventing inflammatory allergic responses in response to pathogens (Mattsby-Baltzer et al. 1996). As a result, breastfeeding is associated with a reduction in inflammatory and autoimmune diseases, helping to prevent immune-system disorders including eczema (Saarinen and Kajosaari 1995), asthma (Bener et al. 2007), and diabetes (Kolb and Pozzilli 1999). If your baby is not breastfed, then other methods can be used to stimulate and augment the immune system and prevent inflammatory conditions.

Babies are born with a sterile gut. They begin to colonize healthy intestinal bacteria at birth in order to digest food and prevent infection. Intestinal bacteria serve a variety of functions, including digestion of carbohydrates, repression of pathogens, promotion of the intestinal lining's production of antibodies, and training the immune system to prevent allergies. If babies receive antibiotics that destroy these beneficial bacteria, then they will need replacement of these bacteria through a probiotic supplement. The cascade of dysfunction that occurs in the gut mucosa as a result of drugs can be addressed through an integrated treatment plan that will reestablish normal digestive and immune-system function.

treatment of immune dysfunction

Most of the problems discussed in the preceding chapters of this book describe different aspects of digestive and immune dysfunction in babies. Sometimes these will manifest as digestive symptoms. At other times they will appear as chronic or recurrent respiratory problems and allergies. Many babies will have a combination of symptoms that may include reflux, eczema, recurrent ear infections, chronic congestion, and asthma. All of these problems can have similar causation. Even though each of these problems has distinct and specific forms of treatment described in previous chapters, they also have similarities in common that a general immune-system treatment plan can address. In this chapter, we'll look at the immune dysfunction that underlies the varied manifestations of symptom expression.

Babies are easily disturbed. Their immune systems are fragile, and they can be set off course by a single stressful jolt to the system. Once they are on the wrong track, it may be difficult for them to recover their equilibrium, especially if symptoms continue to be treated with stressful drugs. One prescription of antibiotics can lead to a downward spiral of recurrent infections, repeated antibiotics, and eventually a chronic health problem. Other babies are more resilient and right themselves if they are thrown off track. For all babies, the more immune-system support they receive, the better the outcome. On the other hand, babies are so resilient and responsive to positive health measures that they do bounce back easily once they're nudged in the right direction. Sometimes the transformation is seemingly miraculous. A simple intervention such as one dose of a homeopathic medicine or even a few doses of an herbal formula can set them on a course of healing that results in full recovery. One or two interventions may be all the support a baby needs to recover her equilibrium. And other times babies require a fully integrated treatment plan to overcome a panoply of interwoven patterns of symptoms and immune dysfunction.

An integrated treatment plan for immune-system problems can be eclectic, and sometimes babies need support from several different directions to get themselves into a healthy state. This plan may include a program of homeopathy, herbs, nutritional support, probiotics, and physical treatment with chiropractic adjustment and acupuncture. Your baby is not likely to need all of these. Taking a slow approach may provide dramatic benefits. The more complex the immune-system problem, the more forms of support may be necessary. But once your baby has recovered immune-system integrity, she will probably maintain this healthy balance.

The Gut and Immunity

Your baby's digestive tract is immature and delicate. In chapter 2, we saw the problems created by an immature sphincter muscle unable to keep stomach acids in the tummy. Similarly, your baby's intestinal lining is immature and not yet fully formed. This lining creates a barrier that separates the inside of the body and the circulation from the outside world and its foreign proteins and bacteria. However, the barrier in infants is leaky and allows antigens through the intestinal walls. Fortunately, this barrier function is enhanced by IgA antibodies contained in breast milk, which provide a protective coating for the intestinal lining. Breast milk also contains a substance that promotes growth of the cells that line the intestine, *epidermal growth factor*. Nonetheless, there are times when foreign proteins leak through this barrier and stimulate antibody production and allergic reactions.

The lining of the digestive tract also produces its own antibodies, in the form of immunoglobulins, to protect against foreign invaders (antigens, bacteria, and toxins). In fact, 80 percent of the body's immunoglobulin-producing cells are located in the mucosa of the GI tract (Brandtzaeg 1998). These immune-protective tissues secrete two types of immunoglobulin. The first is IgA, which resides on the surface of the cells as a protective layer—a kind of antiseptic paint. This IgA neutralizes viruses and removes antigens. If these invaders penetrate this protective layer, then a second line of defense comes into action, circulating IgE or IgG antibodies. This is a systemic allergic response, with antibody production and activation of inflammation to counteract these invaders. Inflammation destroys these pathogens and foreign proteins, but this inflammatory process can damage the delicate tissues of your baby's intestinal lining.

Restoring the Digestive Tract

The field of functional medicine has developed a simple conceptual system for treating the digestive-tract imbalance that underlies many immune-system problems in babies and older children. This system describes a therapeutic process that evaluates GI function and uses targeted nutrition and digestive support to promote normalization of the digestive-tract structure and function. The principles involve restoration of digestive function using four concepts: *removing* irritants and pathogens, *replacing* enzymes that may be deficient, *reinoculating* with healthy intestinal bacteria to create a balance of flora in the gut, and *repairing and regenerating* the intestinal mucosa with targeted nutritional support. This is known as "the four-R program," and this section of the book describes each of these steps.

Remove Irritants and Pathogens

Infants are easily irritated by foreign proteins in foods. These proteins may stimulate antibody production, allergic reactions, and inflammation of the digestive lining. Your baby may need a break from these allergens or irritants. These products can be contained in breast milk or formula. Many substances that irritate babies are described in the discussion of reflux in chapter 2. The most common of these are cow's milk, wheat, beans, corn, eggs, and soy. Other substances in breast milk may also be irritants to your baby's digestive tract, including caffeine, spices, chocolate, onions, and garlic. Sometimes your baby's reactions to these foods are obvious, but many times the causative agents will be a mystery that needs unraveling.

The best way to discover the allergens or offending food for a breastfeeding baby is for Mom to avoid the entire list of likely suspects. This process is sometimes called the elimination diet. Then add foods back to your diet one at a time, eating the new food for a few days before adding another. It's possible to also do an elimination diet with older babies who are eating solids and with older children. This process is time-consuming, but the elimination diet will sometimes result in quick improvement of symptoms.

Even an elimination diet may not be successful in alleviating symptoms if allergic reactions have already caused inflammation in the digestive tract, allowing allergens to continue leaking through the injured intestinal lining. Then it will take time and other steps in the four-R program to heal the gut and alleviate symptoms.

Babies and older children can be tested for food allergies and food sensitivities with IgE and IgG blood tests. It may be informative for mothers to have IgG food-sensitivity testing themselves while they are breastfeeding, since mothers and babies often have similar food reactions. These tests will point to foods that may be causing problems, making it a little easier to focus an elimination diet on those suspicious offenders. However, no tests are completely accurate, and there will inevitably be false positive and false negative results. The body may form antibodies to specific foods, but the individual may not have allergic reactions to these foods. The antibodies may be there but not cause symptoms. Foods can also be irritants without causing allergic responses.

Replace Enzymes

Digestive enzymes are produced by the pancreas to break down complex fats, carbohydrates, and proteins into smaller molecules that our bodies can absorb and utilize for nutrition. If digestive enzymes are deficient, as indicated through stool tests or clinical symptoms, these enzymes may need to be replaced through supplementation. Typical symptoms of enzyme deficiency are bloating and flatulence two to four hours after eating. Digestive-enzyme deficiency will apply mostly to older children. For example, lactose intolerance due to inadequate production of the enzyme lactase is rare in infants but common in children after weaning. Approximately 70 percent of the world's population develops an inability to digest lactose, the sugar in milk. In many ethnic groups, lactose intolerance commonly develops after the age of four to ten years old. Nearly 100 percent of Asians and Native Americans and 60 to 80 percent of Hispanics and African-Americans have lactose intolerance. Approximately 20 percent of Hispanic, African-American, and Asian children will develop lactose intolerance prior to five years of age compared to white children, who do not usually develop problems digesting lactose until after five years of age (Heyman 2006). This is presumed to be a result of the variability in exposure to dairy products in different cultures and genetic selection of individuals with an ability to digest lactose in those cultures. A study of the molecular basis for lactase activity demonstrated that Thai children lost the ability to digest lactose at one to two years of age compared to Finnish children, who had persistent lactase activity until at least ten to twenty years of age (Wang et al. 1998). Some babies who develop severe viral diarrhea during infancy will also develop lactose intolerance. In this case, the inflammation of the intestinal lining destroys the cells that produce lactase in the gut.

The diagnosis of lactose intolerance is usually made in cases where symptoms begin soon after eating dairy products. Avoidance of dairy products or taking lactase when dairy products are consumed will usually prevent the symptoms associated with lactose intolerance. And some individuals may be able to tolerate small amounts of lactose, especially in yogurt or cheese, and develop symptoms only after consuming larger quantities of dairy products, especially milk.

Other digestive-enzyme activity can be evaluated through stool testing available through several labs (Genova, Metametrix, Diagnos-Techs; see appendix 2). Children with low digestive-enzyme levels may benefit from taking a digestive-enzyme supplement.

The production of digestive enzymes can improve over time as other forms of holistic treatment stimulate healthy digestive function. Then the replacement phase of supplementation can be reduced and eventually stopped.

Reinoculate with Healthy Intestinal Bacteria

Reinoculation refers to the reintroduction of healthy intestinal bacteria or probiotics into the digestive tract. Giving babies a probiotic supplement may be the single most important intervention they receive in a therapeutic regimen. Establishing normal flora in the intestines serves many functions. The most important is that probiotics provide desirable bacteria that create an environment hostile to pathogenic bacteria. Colonization with healthy bacterial species is associated with a reduction in diarrheal disease in babies and enhancement of the immune function of the intestines. Probiotics also synthesize vitamins and produce short-chain fatty acids that stimulate cell growth and function. They also degrade toxins and facilitate lactose digestion in lactose-intolerant individuals.

The primary bacteria present in the gut of breastfed babies are *Bifidobacterium* species. When your baby eats solid food or receives any formula, then *Lactobacillus* species begin to proliferate as well.

When these health-promoting intestinal bacteria are deficient, for example when antibiotics have destroyed them, then other pathogens can proliferate and the intestinal lining may become irritated. This state of intestinal-bacteria imbalance is known as dysbiosis.

Breastfeeding infants will benefit from a probiotic formula that stresses or provides only *Bifidobacterium*, with the assumption that these colonies have not adequately proliferated on their own, and older babies need a spectrum of *Bifidobacterium* and *Lactobacillus*. In addition, specific species of these bacteria have been found to be beneficial for different health problems in babies, and these are discussed in detail in the corresponding chapters in this book. For example, *Lactobacillus reuteri* has proven especially applicable to allergic reactions and reflux.

Saccharomyces boulardii is a type of yeast categorized as a probiotic. It does not colonize the gut but acts directly to discourage pathogens. When given as a supplement, *S. boulardii* inhibits harmful bacteria in the intestine and stimulates the secretion of secretory IgA, which protects the intestinal mucosa. *S. boulardii* inhibits and antagonizes candida yeast overgrowth. If problems with yeast are suspected, either because of symptoms in the form of thrush and recurrent yeast diaper rashes or because of candida growth in stool cultures, then a supplement containing *S. boulardii* is indicated.

Certain nutrients serve as fuel for your baby's healthy intestinal bacteria (*Lactobacillus* and *Bifidobacterium*). These nutrients are sugars referred to as prebiotics. The primary prebiotics for supplement use occur in the form of fructooligosaccharides (FOS) derived from vegetables and fruits and arabinogalactans found in echinacea, carrots, radishes, pears, wheat, and tomatoes. Both types of sugars increase populations of beneficial intestinal bacteria. Arabinogalactans also support immune function by stimulating white blood cell activity (Kelly 1999).

A healthy intestine colonized by beneficial bacteria results in a healthy intestinal lining and a vigorous and efficient immune system. By contrast, when intestinal populations of *Lactobacillus* and *Bifidobacterium* become deficient, due to either antibiotic exposure or intestinal diseases and accompanying diarrhea, then pathogenic bacteria and yeast can take hold and cause inflammation, injury of the intestinal lining, abnormal permeability (the ability of antigens to escape into the bloodstream), allergic reactions, and further inflammation of the gut lining. When these bacteria are replaced through supplementation and nourished with prebiotics, then the previous damage is repaired and normal function of the intestinal lining can be reestablished, resulting in a healthy and balanced immune system.

Repair and Regenerate the Intestinal Mucosa

The fourth R in the program involves supplements that provide support for the healing, repair, and regeneration of the intestinal lining. A variety of supplements can soothe and repair the inflammatory process that occurs in the intestine. For babies, one of the most beneficial supplements for intestinal inflammation is the amino acid L-glutamine (usually referred to simply as glutamine). This important nutrient improves secretory IgA production in the intestinal mucosa. Glutamine also nourishes and induces growth of the cells that line the intestine, repairing the damage caused by inflammation.

Several substances found in whey protein powder and colostrum powder directly benefit the intestinal lining. Lactoferrin is a protein found in milk products and is naturally secreted by mucosal cells in response to inflammation. Taken as a supplement, lactoferrin has both antibacterial and anti-inflammatory effects on the intestinal lining (Conneely 2001). Other substances in whey include lactoperoxidase and immunoglobulins that provide antimicrobial and antioxidant effects.

One other issue that sometimes causes symptoms in babies and more often in older children is the presence of pathogenic bacteria in the stomach and intestines. When bacteria congregate on mucous membranes, they produce a protective *biofilm* (a matrix of polysaccharides, like the film that builds up on your teeth overnight, which is also a biofilm). This film surrounds the bacterial colonies, protecting them against attack by antibiotics and by the immune system's defense mechanisms. This dynamic sometimes leads to chronic and recurrent infections (Costerton, Stewart, and Greenberg 1999). Several natural supplements can help to break down these biofilms. The most effective biofilm disruptors are digestive enzymes, including cellulase, peptidases, and proteases, which disrupt the structures of biofilms. Prebiotics and probiotics have also shown an ability to disrupt biofilms by displacing the pathogenic bacterial colonies at their attachment sites on mucous membranes (Lee et al. 2003). Once these protective biofilms are disrupted, then the body's own defenses and herbs with antibiotic properties can work more effectively to destroy bacteria and reestablish healthy flora in mucous membranes.

Chinese Medicine

Although classical Chinese medicine does not specifically acknowledge the immune system as a separate entity, the energetic-system theory of Chinese medicine creates a framework for understanding resistance to illness. Chinese medicine does conceptualize Wei Qi, a protective shield that wards off attack by external pathogenic influences, and specific formulas of herbs have been developed to fortify Wei Qi. The most notable of these is Jade Screen (Yu Ping Feng Wan), likened to a screen that protects the body from invasion. Astragalus (Huang Qi) is the primary ingredient of this formula and others like it. Astragalus has antiviral, antioxidant, and anti-inflammatory effects. Its antioxidant effect supports the integrity of mucous membranes in the respiratory tract. It also promotes interferon activity and T-cell function, two mechanisms responsible for cell-mediated immunity. Studies have documented the ability of astragalus to increase IgA and IgG production and enhance white blood cell function. A pediatric variation of this formula has been developed and is known as Children's Jade Defense (Dr. Jake Fratkin's Herbal Formulas). This formula builds Ying Qi (Nutrient Qi derived from air and food) and Wei Qi (Protective Qi), the body's defense system. And other herbs in the formula distribute Wei Qi to protect the exterior against pathogens.

When the immune system is compromised at deeper levels and chronic problems develop such as allergies, asthma, and systemic yeast overgrowth, then a deeper-acting formula is needed. The combination of astragalus and medicinal mushrooms can serve this function. Resilience (CMW) is a formula that combines four mushrooms that have immune-modulating effects with the herb astragalus. This formula nurtures deep levels of Qi sources in the body, replenishing Postnatal Qi and providing tonification of the body's energetic systems in situations of depletion, inflammation, and immune dysregulation.

Since immune function depends upon a healthy digestive tract, using herbal formulas that ensure stability and strength of digestive function can provide a strong foundation for immune-system health. Often the digestive tract is injured and requires nourishment and repair. A Chinese herbal formula that supports digestion (in Chinese terms, the Stomach and Spleen) is often indicated for babies. The pediatric formula Grow and Thrive (CMW) contains herbs that nourish and support the Stomach/Spleen network, tonify Qi, and protect against invasion by pathogens. The formula encourages absorption of nutrients and the movement of food through the digestive tract, treating constipation and preventing diarrhea in babies. Once the Stomach/Spleen system is strengthened, then Postnatal Qi, Nutritive Qi, and Protective Qi (Wei Qi) all become fortified.

Nutritional Supplements

Several categories of supplements have the ability to support immune function through a range of different mechanisms. Some will support immune activity in the gut and others will have a more generalized protective and nutritive effect.

Vitamin D3

One of the most important nutrients in building immune function independent of the digestive system is vitamin D3 (chole-calciferol). Your baby may produce adequate amounts of vitamin D3 on her own if her skin is exposed to the sun. I recommend ten to twenty minutes a day during the summer months if she is light skinned and forty-five to sixty minutes a day if she is dark skinned (Matsuoka et al. 1991). This also implies that the sun exposure occurs at midday between ten a.m. and two p.m., when UVB rays are strongest. At other times of the year, supplementation with vitamin D3 is necessary to maintain a vital immune system if you live north of 30 degrees north latitude (the level of San Diego, New Orleans, and Cairo).

Vitamin D3 serves a dual purpose of promoting immune function and preventing inflammation. Children with recurrent infections and children with allergies and asthma will all benefit from maintaining adequate vitamin D3 levels. Individuals with normal vitamin D3 levels tend to have fewer viral infections than people with low vitamin D3 levels. The daily requirement of vitamin D3 is 1,000 IU in babies and 2,000 IU in older children. Giving your baby a supplement of vitamin D3 in liquid form will ensure the supply of this vital nutrient.

Colostrum

Colostrum is a nearly magical substance. Breastfeeding babies receive the benefits of colostrum in the first few days after their birth, and many of the immune-enhancing properties in breast milk are similar to those in colostrum. If your baby begins nursing less often, weans from breastfeeding, or must have formula, then consider using cow's colostrum as a supplement to boost immunity.

Colostrum contains a host of factors that stimulate the immune system and help to prevent illness. The immunoglobulin IgA coats the intestinal lining, preventing attack by pathogens. Lactoferrin locks onto iron, releasing it to red blood cells and depriving bacteria of the iron they need for reproduction. Lysozymes are enzymes that destroy microorganisms on contact. Cytokines are signaling proteins that boost T-cell activity and stimulate production of your baby's own protective immunoglobulins. Polysaccharides are carbohydrates that bind to bacteria and block their attachment to mucous membranes.

Powdered colostrum from cows raised in New Zealand on pesticide-free pastures is available from Sedona Labs, Symbiotics, and other suppliers. Flavored chewable colostrum tablets are also manufactured for older children.

Fish Oil

The anti-inflammatory effect of omega-3 fats found in fish oil is well documented and has led most nutritionists to recommend fish oil for everyone. The omega-3 fatty acid EPA has anti-inflammatory effects and the omega-3 fatty acid DHA is essential for normal and enhanced neurological development and brain function of children. Both of these fatty acids are richly supplied in fish and fish oil. However, I do not recommend that children eat any fish except wild salmon and other small wild fish from unpolluted sources. Farmed fish is contaminated with pesticides and antibiotics unless they are raised in organic fisheries. Other ocean fish contain unacceptably high levels of mercury. Other animal products may contain omega-3 fats, such as eggs from chickens that are fed green foods or flax, but a large percentage of the omega-3 fats may be in the form of ALA, which is not readily utilized. Meat may contain significant amounts of EPA and DHA if the animals are fed green products, as is the case for truly grass-fed cattle.

All reputable commercial manufacturers of fish oil test their products to ensure they are free from contamination by toxic metals and pesticide residues, so there is no concern about any possible toxic effects of fish oil as a supplement. There is concern about depleting the world's supply of fish. For this reason, it is best to use fish oil from small fish such as anchovies and sardines. Breast milk will supply babies with omega-3 fats if mothers take adequate amounts of a supplement that contains at least 2,000 mg EPA and 1,000 mg DHA from fish oil. An alternative source of omega-3 fats for adults is krill oil, which is more readily absorbed than fish oil and does not deplete fish populations. Since krill oil has an enhanced absorption and antioxidant quality compared to fish oil, you can take one-third to one-half the usual dosage of fish oil. Because of its fishy taste, krill is not the most palatable source of omega-3 fats for babies.

Cod-liver oil is another possible source of omega-3 fats and also contains vitamins A and D. However, almost all cod-liver oil supplements are prepared by processing that removes the vitamins A and D3 contained in the liver of fish and then adds them back to the oil in varying amounts. There is also some concern that vitamin A can interfere with the absorption of vitamin D3, and most people eating a natural-foods diet rich in vegetables and fruits do get adequate amounts of vitamin A. Because of these concerns, it is probably better to use fish oil as a supplement for your baby.

Flaxseed oil is sometimes recommended as a source of omega-3 fats, but flax and other plant sources of omega-3 fats, such as hemp, contain the fatty acid ALA, which must be converted to the usable forms EPA and DHA by an enzymatic process in the body. Babies do not reliably produce this enzyme, and so they may not get the benefit of the omega-3 fat from flax oil.

A vegetarian source of DHA produced from algae under the brand name Neuromins is also available. This form of DHA is supplied in capsules, usually of 100 mg. You can puncture the capsule and give it to your baby that way, but there are no reliable vegetarian sources of EPA in supplement form.

The dosage of omega-3 fats is 200 to 500 mg each of EPA and DHA per day for babies, or at least 32 mg per pound of body weight of EPA plus DHA (thus a twenty-pound baby will need about 600 mg total of these omega-3 fats).

Probiotics

I've discussed the use of probiotics for healthy gut and immune function in other areas of this book. Research has shown that *Lactobacillus* and *Bifidobacterium* strains support immune function in many ways. One study evaluated the effect of *Lactobacillus acidophilus* NCFM and *Bifidobacterium lactis* Bi-07 strains on immune function in children. That study showed that children aged three to five years given these probiotics during the winter months had significantly fewer illnesses with fever, cough, and runny nose compared to a control group. Cough was reduced by 54 percent, fever incidence was reduced by 63 percent, and antibiotic use was reduced by 80 percent in the children given the two probiotics (Ouwehand, Leyer, and Carcano 2008). Another study showed that babies from four to twelve months old who received *Lactobacillus reuteri* had a lower incidence of diarrhea and fever than the control group (Weizman, Asli, and Alsheikh 2005). In another study, *Lactobacillus plantarum* reduced the incidence of diarrhea in a day care center when diarrhea was rampant (Ribeiro and Vanderhoof 1998). Probiotics have proven effective in reducing other contagious illnesses as well, including acute viral diarrhea in infants and traveler's diarrhea.

These studies show the protective effect of probiotic supplementation for prevention of illness in infants and the utility of a broad-spectrum infant probiotic supplement · for improving immune function in babies who seem to have lowered resistance to infections.

Homeopathic Medicine

Of all the mysterious and seemingly magical effects of holistic treatment, homeopathy is the most impressive and the most difficult to understand. Unlike Chinese medicine, which has a vast theoretical underpinning to elucidate its effects, homeopathy is based on a very simple assumption that seems strange to our modern ears: give a medicine that is capable of causing symptoms similar to those of the disease. Homeopathic medicines are prescribed in amazingly small doses, in infinitesimal dilutions. Often a single medicine is given in a single dose. Acceptance of homeopathic treatment is an act of blind faith or trust by parents, who are often desperate to find a solution to their baby's symptoms. Nonetheless, homeopathy can have a profound and deeply curative effect on symptoms and the restoration of overall health for your baby.

Homeopathy is best utilized in the context of an overall holistic plan for your baby that includes eating an excellent whole-foods diet, providing nutritional support through appropriate supplements, and minimizing toxic exposure. Homeopathy seems to work by providing a stimulus to healing, using the fabric and foundation of the body's own vitality and healing mechanisms. In babies this vitality is usually abundant, and they respond extraordinarily well to homeopathy. Including constitutional homeopathy in a treatment program often proves miraculous. Given the support of a holistic healing plan, a homeopathic constitutional medicine can stimulate a healing reaction that persists indefinitely. To determine an appropriate and effective constitutional prescription, the entire complex of symptoms and components of your baby's metabolism and history must be taken into account. Only a trained homeopath can provide the expertise necessary for a correct prescription. By contrast, using homeopathic medicines for acute illness is simple and relatively straightforward and can be accomplished successfully by professionals with minimal training and by parents at home.

Homeopathy is especially appropriate for problems that involve immune function because homeopathy works first at energetic levels of the body. Functional problems such as inflammation, allergic responses, digestive motility, and mucus production are readily turned on and off by the body. Given the correct stimulus, it is theoretically possible for these types of symptoms to improve overnight. Homeopathy can provide that trigger.

When the body is functioning at a high level of performance, then problems brought on by stress or genetic predispositions often improve. The inner ecology of the body often determines the expression of symptoms and disease. Genetic expression can be turned on and off. Homeopathy is an excellent way to trigger this kind of quick reversal. Then the work of repair can begin, supported by a whole-foods diet and the proper nutrients.

Homeopathy has limitations where structural problems predominate or cause symptoms. A gut lining that is damaged by inflammation takes time to heal with any type of treatment, but a hyperreactive mucous membrane can be calmed immediately.

There are many permutations of the interaction between structure and function. Each individual child will have a different expression of a particular disease process in terms of structural integrity and breakdown, between functional energetic balance and chemical deficiency. The art of a holistic approach to illness involves this interplay between support of structure and tissue integrity and adequate nutrient availability on one hand, and the energetic stimulus to recreate balance provided by a homeopathic medicine or an acupuncture needle on the other. Either approach may work on its own: the functional-medicine support of tissue function and body chemistry or the energetic stimulus of home-opathy. But together, these two provide a remarkable synergy. The same is true of homeopathy and Chinese medicine. Where home-opathy has the ability to provide the big bang and catalyze a tre-mendous healing reaction, Chinese medicine is able to mold and shape symptom expression and energetic balance in the body. The two often serve different functions, but they can be used harmo-niously in a holistic fashion to arrive at a desired conclusion: the rebuilding of health and actual cure.

■ Case Report ■
Immune Dysfunction

A ten-month-old boy I'll call Jack, who had previously suf-fered from nearly every health problem described in this book, came to see me with his father. As an infant, he had chronic and persistent nasal congestion. At the same time, he had recurrent burping and vomiting. His diges-tive problems disappeared on their own, but he was diag-nosed with two episodes of bronchiolitis with wheezing, and he had been prescribed a bronchodilator, levalbuterol. He continued to have a cough after these episodes, and when I first saw him he had been coughing at night for the preceding two months. Whenever he went outside he sneezed and developed a runny nose. His father also had asthma. Jack was diagnosed twice with ear infections and persistent fluid in the middle ear.

He was a happy, relaxed, playful baby, usually in good spirits. He was independent and would play on his own for long periods of time. He was also persistent and a little stubborn. He knew what he wanted and would cry until he got it. His only other notable symptom was significant head sweats, often a sign of allergies in babies, and a characteristic that helped lead to the prescription of his homeopathic medicine.

In his initial treatment program, I included a homeopathic constitutional medicine, *Calcarea carbonica* 1M. A Chinese herbal combination that included the formulas Grow and Thrive and Deep Breath to build immune function, address the digestive component, and treat the chronic cough was the other primary treatment. I addressed secondary issues with the supplements vitamin D3 at 1,200 IU daily, fish oil (1 teaspoon a day), a probiotic formula of *Bifidobacterium* and *Lactobacillus* species, and colostrum powder.

Jack steadily improved after this treatment regimen. His cough disappeared, and he was no longer clearing his throat of constant drainage. He had no recurrence of ear infections, wheezing, or digestive problems.

■ ■

summary

During the second half of the first year of life, the immune system is really the big news for your baby's state of health. Most visits to doctors, most recurrent problems, and most of the drugs given to babies revolve around immune-system issues. Babies get into all sorts of trouble because of their immune systems. They get sick too often, they develop mysterious forms of congestion, allergies, and persistent coughs and wheezing. And these problems, left untreated, can and often do persist for years. Yet the treatment of these problems is relatively simple. Their cure is within reach, and so much needless suffering and many sleepless nights can be saved with a few interventions. Even though the assessment of causes and the evaluation of this immune-system breakdown can be complicated, just instituting some simple steps can reverse a downward spiral that has frustrated parents for months.

Give your baby the best diet possible. Whenever possible, breastfeed for at least the first year. Feed your baby organic, whole foods free of petrochemicals and pesticides. Prepare your own whole fresh foods and juices as much as you can, and avoid processed and packaged foods, including juices and baby foods in jars.

Correct the damage done to the digestive tract and restore its normal function. This is often the first step to health because most immune function originates in the gut. Using probiotics and prebiotics will establish a healthy environment. Giving a few nutrients for healthy digestive function will help heal any damage done to cells in the intestinal lining. Supporting immune mechanisms with vitamin D3, fish oil, colostrum, or whey protein powder will provide nourishment, prevent inflammation, and build immune-system strength.

Use herbs that build the support system for immune function. Strengthen the Stomach/Spleen network and Wei Qi (Protective Qi) with Chinese herbal formulas. Give a constitutional homeopathic medicine to provide a stimulus to healing.

Providing proper nutrition and supporting the immune system represents an excellent preventive program for all babies. Developing a holistic healing plan as described in this book and with the help of a qualified holistic health professional will improve your baby's immune function and resolve the range of problems we have discussed.

immune-system support

Probiotics and prebiotics

Digestive enzymes

Glutamine

Whey powder or colostrum

Vitamin D3 (cholecalciferol)

Fish oil

Chinese herbs—Children's Jade Defense (Dr. Jake Fratkin) or Grow and Thrive (CMW)

Mushroom formulas

APPENDIX 1

- - - - - - - - - -

medications and supplements

This appendix provides more specific information about some of the medications and supplements I introduced in the book. Here you'll find information about dosages and where to obtain these products.

- -

nutritional supplements

Supplements come packaged in various forms, including oils, liquid extracts, gel caps, powders, and capsules containing powder. Gel caps can be punctured and the contents given directly in your baby's mouth or mixed with food. Powders can be mixed with breast milk or other foods, and the contents of capsules can be emptied into your baby's food as well. For older babies, you can prepare a smoothie in the blender with fruit and water or rice milk and add supplements to that.

Some suppliers sell their products to consumers at health food stores or online through their website or distributors' sites. Other manufacturers will only sell products to licensed health care practitioners. Your baby's medical provider can order these products for you. I have provided some suggestions for specific manufacturers, especially when a supplement may be harder to find.

Dosage Calculation

If you know the adult dose of a supplement, there are two formulas that will help you calculate the appropriate child's dose:

1. **By weight:** Divide the weight of the child (in pounds) by 150 to give the approximate fraction of the adult dose. For instance, if your baby is 20 pounds, divide 20 by 150. This will equal 13, meaning the appropriate dose is 13 percent of the adult dose.

2. **By age:** Divide the age of the child in years by the age of the child plus twelve to give the fraction of the adult dose. For example, if your child is 3 years old, you would add 3 and 12 and then divide 3 by the resulting number (15). So, 3 divided by 15 will equal .20. Therefore, you would give your child 20 percent of the adult dose.

Fish Oil

Fish oil contains the important omega-3 fatty acids EPA and DHA. These fats are important for growth, prevention and treatment of inflammation, and nervous-system development and function. Fish oil can be given as an oil to babies or in capsules to older children. There are many manufacturers of fish oil, and as long as they guarantee that their product is free of metal and pesticide contamination, then they are safe for your baby.

EPA dosage: 200-500 mg/day

DHA dosage: 200-500 mg/day

Gamma-Linolenic Acid

GLA is an important fatty acid for treating eczema and other skin problems (cradle cap) in children who may not convert linoleic acid to GLA because of an enzyme deficiency. It is available from borage-seed oil or evening primrose oil supplements.

GLA dosage: 200-250 mg/day

L-Glutamine

L-Glutamine is an amino acid that nourishes and heals the cells of the intestinal lining.

L-Glutamine dosage: about 200 mg/day

Prebiotics

Prebiotics include fructooligosaccharides (FOS) and arabinogalactan (from larch) to support probiotic growth. Here are some recommended prebiotic formulas:

- Probioplex Intensive Care by Metagenics contains FOS plus immune-system stimulants. It is available at www.metagenics.com.

- BiotaGen by Klaire Laboratories is a similar formula with FOS and arabinogalactan and is available at www.klaire.com.

- FOS by Pure Encapsulations (www.purecaps.com) contains a specifically formulated probiotic-enhancing formula.

Probiotics

Probiotics are beneficial intestinal bacteria. Many different products are available that contain varying potencies and varying combinations of probiotic strains. A high "colony count" is preferred (the higher the count, the more bacteria are present). Many products also contain prebiotics in the form of inulin, various polysaccharides, and oligosaccharides, especially those from Klaire (www.klaire.com) to stimulate intestinal bacteria colonization.

- *Lactobacillus* and *Bifidobacterium* species are available in a broad-spectrum combination as Ther-Biotic Infant Formula by Klaire, BifidoBiotics by Allergy Research Group (www.allergyresearchgroup.com), and many other formulations.

- *Bifidobacterium* species alone are available as Ther-Biotic Factor 4 by Klaire.

- A combination of *L. reuteri* and *L. rhamnosus* with other strains and FOS is available as Primadophilus by Nature's Way (www.naturesway.com).

- A combination of *L. acidophilus* NCFM and *B. lactis* Bi-07 with FOS is available as Ultra Flora Plus DF by Metagenics at www.metagenics.com.

- *Saccharomyces boulardii* is available alone from Klaire or combined with the other probiotics *L. rhamnosus* and *B. lactis* and the prebiotic FOS as Proboulardi by Metagenics (www.metagenics.com).

Vitamin D3

Vitamin D3 (cholecalciferal) is essential for immune-system function. The daily dosage is 1,000 IU for babies and 2,000 IU for preschoolers and older. Do not use vitamin D2 (ergocalciferol), a synthetic form which may have toxicity. Here are some sources for quality formulations of vitamin D3:

- Liquid drops from Biotics Research Corporation at www.bioticsresearch.com (Bio-D-Mulsion, 400 IU/drop; Bio-D-Mulsion Forte, 2,000 IU/drop).

- Chewable vitamin D3, 1,000 IU for available from Pharmax at www.pharmaxllc.com. Because it comes in a tablet form, this supplement is only appropriate for older babies who have molars they can use to chew.

homeopathic medicines

Using homeopathy for your baby's acute conditions is really simple. Once you have found the correct remedy (using the indications in this book or other books that describe the medicines), then get the remedy from a health-food store or online supplier. Many homeopathic pharmacies also carry home kits of commonly used homeopathic medicines for acute illness. You can purchase one of these and then have your own set of medicines to use at home as the occasion arises.

The numbers and letters following the name of a homeopathic medicine signify the pharmaceutical method and strength of the preparation. You can use a 6, 12, or 30 strength of each medicine. These numbers refer to the number of times the product has been diluted by the pharmacy. Paradoxically, the more dilutions, the stronger the medicine. Many outlets such as health-food stores and some pharmacies carry homeopathic medicines, and they will stock one or more of these dosages. The strength of the medicine is really unimportant for our purposes.

The vials of medicines will also be labeled with an X or C (6X or 6C, 30X or 30C), denoting the method of dilution by the pharmacy—either 1:10 for X or 1:100 for C. Sometimes the letters CH or CK will appear, which are the same as C. And sometimes you will see D or DH, which are the same as X. Really, the only important issue for your purposes is getting the name of the medicine right. The names are always in Latin, for the plant, mineral, or animal product used to prepare the medicine.

Homeopathic medicines are dispensed on sugar pellets and packaged in vials. The pellets have been saturated with the liquid homeopathic preparation of the original substance. This is simply an easy form to take. Children love their sweet taste. The number of pellets you give is unimportant. You can give one, two, or three pellets as a dose. Homeopathic medicines are nontoxic and over-dosing is not possible.

After choosing what you think is the correct remedy, give your baby a dose. For young babies, the best way to do this is to grind up the medicine and dissolve in water or milk. Older children who have molars can chew them up. Observe the effect of the first dose. With homeopathic medicines, sometimes one dose is all that's required. The homeopathic medicine works by stimulating a healing response. Once that response occurs, it may continue without further treatment. For example, if your baby has teething pain and you give a dose of *Chamomilla*, the pain may disappear. If your baby gets fussy again with obvious teething pain, repeat the dose. The rule is, as long as symptoms are improving, you don't need to repeat the medicine. If symptoms continue, then you can repeat the dose. The interval of repetition will depend on the severity of symptoms. The more severe the symptoms, the more frequently you should repeat the medicine. For example, for a baby having a difficult time breathing, you can repeat the medicine every ten to fifteen minutes. For most illnesses (like colds and coughs), you will probably want to give a dose of the medicine every three or four hours.

Chronic problems such as eczema or asthma require the care of a trained and experienced homeopathic practitioner, who may use other types of remedy preparations or dosage schedules that are more appropriate to these conditions.

chinese herbal formulas

Most pediatric formulas discussed in this book are prepared in liquid extracts and preserved with glycerin or alcohol. Each formula is usually a combination of ten or more individual herbs that have been cooked together to comprise a balanced prescription. All of the formulas cited are nontoxic. They cannot hurt your child, and they have all been tested for contaminants, pesticides, and heavy metals. They are designed for pediatric use. The amount of alcohol in the pediatric formulas is kept at a low level, but it can be removed before giving it to your baby. Simply place the drops in a small amount of boiling water, allow it to cool, and the alcohol will be burned off.

The dosage of Chinese herbal formulas will depend upon the individual formula, the child's age, and the severity of symptoms. Generally, most formulas are repeated more often for flare-ups of symptoms or acute illnesses, usually every two to three hours. For liquid extracts in acute situations, two to three full droppers at a time may be necessary. For maintenance therapy, twice a day is usually a sufficient regimen. The dosage of herbs will vary by manufacturer, but generally one full dropper twice a day for infants and two droppers twice a day for toddlers will be adequate.

Trained Chinese herbalists may choose to use classical formulas in powder or granular form, but these prescriptions require a high level of expertise. The dosage will depend upon the individual formula and the condition of the child. Herbalists may choose to use one of these manufactured formulas, or they may prepare the powder mixture themselves to individualize the prescription. At other times, herbalists will prescribe more than one liquid formula or mix them together to arrive at the best combination of herbs for your child.

Since the use of Chinese herbs requires training and expertise in the practice of Chinese medicine, many manufacturers will only provide their products to licensed health care professionals. If you do not have access to a Chinese herbal practitioner, then your own health care provider may be willing to work with you to prescribe these pediatric herbal formulas utilizing the guidelines outlined in this book.

- - - - - - - - - - -

further resources
for parents

- -

books

While *The Holistic Baby Guide* provides the essential information you need to begin to treat your baby's health problems in a holistic way, you may be interested in learning more. The titles that follow will be helpful resources for more information about some of the topics I have discussed in this book. You may want to add these to your library for reference.

Baby Care

Child Health Guide: Holistic Pediatrics for Parents, by Randall Neustaedter (North Atlantic Books, 2005, 320 pages). The definitive guide to raising a healthy child from birth through adolescence using the most natural methods of parenting, including healthy diets, attachment parenting styles, holistic treatments at home for common acute conditions, and avoidance of toxins.

The Baby Book: Everything You Need to Know About Your Baby from Birth to Age Two, by William and Martha Sears (Little, Brown, and Company, 2003, 704 pages). One of the best how-to baby books, with a baby-centered approach to promoting attachment. Good advice about raising your baby but, unfortunately, conventional medical advice about illnesses and symptoms.

Attachment Parenting: Instinctive Care for Your Baby and Young Child, by Katie Allison Granju (Atria, 1999, 336 pages). This classic describes the principles of listening to your baby's needs and trusting your instincts.

Nutrition

The Breastfeeding Book, by Martha and William Sears (Little, Brown, 2000, 272 pages). Everything you need to be successful, with an emphasis on bed sharing, attachment parenting, and extended breastfeeding.

The Ultimate Breastfeeding Book of Answers, by Jack Newman and Teresa Pitman (Prima Lifestyles, 2000, 464 pages). This guide takes you through all the steps necessary to establish a healthy breastfeeding relationship and answers an amazing number of practical, obscure, and unusual questions about breastfeeding details.

Nourishing Traditions: The Cookbook That Challenges Politically Correct Nutrition and the Diet Dictocrats, by Sally Fallon with Mary Enig (New Trends Publishing, 2001, 670 pages). Not just for kids' diets, but an entire way of eating that includes appropriate levels of fats, protein, and sprouted grains as the keystones for a healthy diet. This is the book I can wholeheartedly recommend for family nutrition.

Homeopathy

The American Institute of Homeopathy Handbook for Parents, by Edward Shalts (Jossey-Bass, 2005, 365 pages). A primer about homeopathy and a guide to the use of homeopathic medicine for children's acute and chronic diseases and syndromes.

Everybody's Guide to Homeopathic Medicines, by Dana Ullman and Stephen Cummings (J. P. Tarcher, 1997, 374 pages). A classic for quick homeopathic prescribing for acute ailments.

Homeopathic Medicine for Children and Infants, by Dana Ullman (J. P. Tarcher, 1992, 256 pages). Another classic, this one focusing on children and infants.

Homeopathic Self-Care: The Quick and Easy Guide for the Whole Family, by Robert Ullman and Judyth Reichenberg-Ullman (Prima Publishing, 1997, 433 pages). A homeopathic home prescriber with step-by-step instructions and visual presentations guiding you to choose the correct medicine.

Asthma

Natural Relief for Your Child's Asthma: A Guide to Controlling Symptoms and Reducing Your Child's Dependence on Drugs, by Steven J. Bock, Kenneth Bock, and Nancy P. Bruning (Harper Perennial, 1999, 285 pages). A useful guide to childhood asthma that outlines a holistic plan, especially for older children.

finding a holistic health care provider

Pediatric Specialists

Holistic Pediatric Association: Alliance for Family Health and Wellness
A professional membership association of pediatric specialists
www.hpakids.org

International Chiropractic Pediatric Association
Chiropractors trained in the holistic treatment of children
www.icpa4kids.com

General Medical Providers

American Holistic Medical Association
A directory of doctors who have an interest in holistic medicine
www.holisticmedicine.org

Council for Homeopathic Certification
Directory of practitioners who have passed a national certification exam in classical homeopathy
www.homeopathicdirectory.com

National Center for Homeopathy
A directory of practitioners who identify themselves as homeopaths
www.nationalcenterforhomeopathy.org

American Association of Acupuncture and Oriental Medicine
A directory of acupuncturists
www.aaaomonline.org

Acufinder.com
A directory of acupuncturists
www.acufinder.com

manufacturers of Chinese herbal formulas

The pediatric formulas we discussed in this book are available to licensed health care providers. These manufacturers are all reliable and safe. They provide regular testing of their formulas for contaminants, including heavy metals and pesticides. Your baby's medical provider can order these for you.

Blue Poppy Pediatric Formulas at www.bluepoppy.com

Chinese Medicine Works Formulas (CMW) including Gentle Warriors, Sage Solutions, and Chinese Modular Solutions at www.kanherb.com

Golden Flower Herbs at www.gfcherbs.com

Dr. Jake Fratkin's Herbal Formulas at www.drjakepaul fratkin.com

testing laboratories

Some of the laboratory testing I described in this book may be new to you and your health care providers. Here I have included websites for some labs that provide the tests I have discussed so that you can investigate them further and discuss them with your baby's medical provider. Both stool tests and allergy tests can be helpful in deciding the most appropriate treatment program for your baby, helping you achieve a speedy and complete recovery from the kinds of immune-system problems discussed in this book.

Stool Tests

Diagnos-Techs at www.diagnostechs.com

Genova Diagnostics at www.genovadiagnostics.com

Metametrix Clinical Laboratory at www.metametrix.com

IgG Allergy Tests

ALCAT Worldwide/Cell Science Systems at www.alcat.com

Alletess Medical Library at www.foodallergy.com

Genova Diagnostics at www.genovadiagnostics.com

Metametrix Clinical Laboratory at www.metametrix.com

US BioTek Laboratories at www.usbiotek.com

references

Abdullah, B., S. Hassan, D. Sidek, and H. Jaafar. 2006. Adenoid mast cells and their role in the pathogenesis of otitis media with effusion. *Journal of Laryngology and Otology* 120(7):556–60.

Abrahamsson, T., T. Jakobsson, M. Böttcher, M. Fredrikson, M. Jenmalm, B. Björkstén, and G. Oldaeus. 2007. Probiotics in prevention of IgE-associated eczema: A double-blind, randomized, placebo-controlled trial. *Journal of Allergy and Clinical Immunology* 119(5):1174–80.

American Academy of Pediatrics Subcommittee on Management of Acute Otitis Media. 2004. Diagnosis and management of acute otitis media. *Pediatrics* 113(5):1451–65.

Andreassi, M., P. Forleo, A. Di Lorio, S. Masci, G. Abate, and P. Amerio. 1997. Efficacy of gamma-linolenic acid in the treatment of patients with atopic dermatitis. *Journal of Internal Medicine Research* 25(5):266–74.

Asami, D. K., Y. J. Hong, D. M. Barrett, and A. E. Mitchell. 2003. Comparison of the total phenolic and ascorbic acid content of freeze-dried and air-dried marionberry, strawberry, and corn grown using conventional, organic, and sustainable agricultural practices. *Journal of Agricultural and Food Chemistry* 51(5):1237–41.

Ayhan, M., B. Sancak, A. Karaduman, S. Arikan, and S. Sahin. 2007. Colonization of neonate skin by *Malassezia* species: Relationship with neonatal cephalic pustulosis. *Journal of the American Academy of Dermatology* 57(6):1012–18.

Beasley, R., T. Clayton, J. Crane, E. Von Mutius, C. Lai, S. Montefort, and A. Stewart. 2008. Association between paracetamol use in infancy and childhood, and risk of asthma, rhinoconjunctivitis, and eczema in children aged 6–7 years: Analysis from Phase Three of the ISAAC programme. *Lancet* 372(9643):1039–48.

Bener, A., M. S. Ehlayel, S. Alsowaidi, and A. Sabbah. 2007. Role of breast feeding in primary prevention of asthma and allergic diseases in a traditional society. *European Annals of Allergy and Clinical Immunology* 39(10):337–43.

Bernier, V., F. X. Weill, V. Hirigoyen, C. Elleau, A. Feyler, C. Labrèze, J. Sarlangue, G. Chène, B. Couprie, and A. Taïeb. 2002. Skin colonization by *Malassezia* species in neonates: A prospective study and relationship with neonatal cephalic pustulosis. *Archives of Dermatology* 138(2):215–18.

Brandtzaeg, P. 1998. Development and basic mechanisms of human gut immunity. *Nutrition Reviews* 56(1 pt. 2):5–18.

Camargo, C. A., S. Rifas-Shiman, A. Litonjua, J. Rich-Edwards, S. Weiss, D. Gold, K. Kleinman, and M. Gillman. 2007. Maternal intake of vitamin D during pregnancy and risk of recurrent wheeze in children at three years of age. *American Journal of Clinical Nutrition* 85(3):788–95.

Canani, R. B., P. Cirillo, P. Roggero, C. Romano, B. Malamisura, G. Terrin, A. Passariello, F. Manguso, L. Morelli, and A. Guarino. 2006. Therapy with gastric acidity inhibitors increases the risk of acute gastroenteritis and community-based acquired pneumonia in children. *Pediatrics* 117(5):817–20.

Canani, R. B., P. Cirillo, G. Terrin, L. Cesarano, M. I. Spagnuolo, A. De Vincenzo, F. Albano, et al. 2007. Probiotics for treatment of acute diarrhoea in children: Randomised clinical trial of five different preparations. *British Medical Journal* 335(7615):340.

Chatzi, L., G. Apostolaki, I. Bibakis, I. Skypala, V. Bibaki-Liakou, N. Tzanakis, M. Kogevinas, and P. Cullinan. 2007. Protective effect of fruits, vegetables, and the Mediterranean diet on asthma and allergies among children in Crete. *Thorax* 62(8):677–83.

Chatzi, L., M. Torrent, I. Romieu, R. Garcia-Esteban, C. Ferrer, J. Vioque, M. Kogevinas, and J. Sunyer. 2008. Mediterranean diet in pregnancy is protective for wheeze and atopy in childhood. *Thorax* 63(6):483–85.

Childhood Asthma Management Research Group. 2000. Long-term effects of budesonide or nedocromil in children with asthma. *New England Journal of Medicine* 343(15):1054–63.

Cohet, C., S. Cheng, C. MacDonald, M. Baker, S. Foliaki, N. Huntington, J. Douwes, and N. Pearce. 2004. Infections, medication use, and the prevalence of symptoms of asthma, rhinitis, and eczema in childhood. *Journal of Epidemiology and Community Health* 58(10):852–57.

Conneely, O. M. 2001. Antiinflammatory activities of lactoferrin. *Journal of the American College of Nutrition* 20(suppl. 5):389S–95S.

Costerton, J. W., P. S. Stewart, and E. P. Greenberg. 1999. Bacterial biofilms: A common cause of persistent infections. *Science* 284(5418):1318–22.

Daniel, K. T. 2005. *The Whole Soy Story: The Dark Side of America's Favorite Health Food.* Washington, DC: New Trends Publishing.

Dekker, C., R. Dales, S. Bartlett, B. Brunekreef, and H. Zwanenburg. 1991. Childhood asthma and the indoor environment. *Chest* 100(4):922–26.

Enriquez, R., W. Addington, F. Davis, S. Freels, C. Park, R. Hershow, and V. Persky. 2005. The relationship between vaccine refusal and self-report of atopic disease in children. *Journal of Allergy and Clinical Immunology* 115(4):737–44.

Eppig, J. J. 1971. Seborrhea capitis in infants: A clinical experience in allergy therapy. *Annals of Allergy* 29(6):323–24.

Feldman, H., J. L. Paradise, C. A. Dollaghan, T. F. Campbell, D. K. Colborn, D. L. Pitcairn, H. E. Rockette, et al. 2002. Early vs. delayed tube placement for persistent middle-ear effusion (MEE) in the first 3 years of life: Effects on intelligence, receptive language, and auditory processing at age 6 years. Presented at the Pediatric Academic Societies annual meeting, May 4–7, Baltimore, MD.

Fiocchi, A., M. Sala, P. Signoroni, G. Banderali, C. Agostoni, and E. Riva. 1994. The efficacy and safety of gamma-linolenic acid in the treatment of infantile atopic dermatitis. *Journal of Internal Medicine Research* 22(1):24–32.

Flaws, B. 2006. *A Handbook of TCM Pediatrics: A Practitioner's Guide to the Care and Treatment of Common Childhood Diseases.* Boulder, CO: Blue Poppy Press.

Forsyth, J. S., S. A. Ogston, A. Clark, C. D. Florey, and P. W. Howie. 1993. Relation between early introduction of solid food to infants and their weight and illnesses during the first two years of life. *British Medical Journal* 306(6892):444.

Fratkin, J. P. 2004. Ear infections and Chinese medicine. www.hpakids.org/holistic-health/articles/148/1/Ear-Infections-and-Chinese-Medicine. Accessed September 6, 2009.

Friese, K. H., S. Kruse, R. Ludtke, and H. Moeller. 1997. The homoeopathic treatment of otitis media in children: Comparisons with conventional therapy. *International Journal of Clinical Pharmacology and Therapeutics* 35(7):296 301.

Gerard, C. M., K. Harris, and B. Thach. 2002. Spontaneous arousals in supine infants while swaddled and unswaddled during rapid eye movement and quiet sleep. *Pediatrics* 100(6):e70.

Gravel, J. S., I. F. Wallace, and R. J. Ruben. 1996. Auditory consequences of early mild hearing loss associated with otitis media. *Acta Oto-Laryngologica* 116(2):219–21.

Griffin, G., C. A. Flynn, R. E. Bailey, and J. K. Schultz. 2006. Antihistamines and/or decongestants for otitis media with effusion (OME) in children. *Cochrane Database of Systematic Reviews* October 18(4):CD003423.

Guandalini, S. 2008. Probiotics for children with diarrhea: An update. *Journal of Clinical Gastroenterology* 42(suppl. 2):53–57.

Haby, M. M., J. K. Peat, G. B. Marks, A. J. Woolcock, and S. R. Leeder. 2001. Asthma in preschool children: Prevalence and risk factors. *Thorax* 56(8):589–95.

Hahnemann, S. 2007. *The Organon of Medicine.* Trans. R. E. Dudgeon. Whitefish, MT: Kessington Publishing.

Hammaren-Malmi, S., H. Saxen, J. Tarkkanen, and P. S. Mattila. 2005. Adenoidectomy does not significantly reduce the incidence of otitis media in conjunction with the insertion of tympanostomy tubes in children who are younger than four years: A randomized trial. *Pediatrics* 116(1):185–89

Henderson, C. A., J. Taylor, and W. J. Cunliffe. 2000. Sebum excretion rates in mothers and neonates. *British Journal of Dermatology* 142(1):110–11.

Henley, D. V., N. Lipson, K. S. Korach, and C. A. Bloch. 2007. Prepubertal gynecomastia linked to lavender and tea tree oils. *New England Journal of Medicine* 356(5):479–85.

Heyman, M. B. 2006. Lactose intolerance in infants, children, and adolescents. *Pediatrics* 118(3):1279–86.

Hill, D. J., N. Roy, R. G. Heine, C. S. Hosking, D. E. Francis, J. Brown, B. Speirs, J. Sadowsky, and J. B. Carlin. 2005. Effect of a low-allergen maternal diet on colic among breastfed infants: A randomized, controlled trial. *Pediatrics* 116(5):e709–15.

Hodge, L., C. M. Salome, J. K. Peat, M. M. Haby, W. Xuan, and A. J. Woolcock. 1996. Consumption of oily fish and childhood asthma risk. *Medical Journal of Australia* 164(3):135–36.

Horrobin, D. F. 2000. Essential fatty acid metabolism and its modification in atopic eczema. *American Journal of Clinical Nutrition* 71(suppl. 1):367–72.

Houghton, H. C. 1875. Catarrhal inflammation of middle ear (ninety-three cases). *Homeopathic Times* i:24.

———.1885. *Lectures on Clinical Otology.* Boston: Otis Clapp & Sons.

Hunziker, U. A., and R. G. Barr. 1986. Increased carrying reduces infant crying: A randomized, controlled trial. *Pediatrics* 77(5):641–48.

Hurwitz, E. L. and H. Morgenstern. 2000. Effects of diphtheria-tetanus-pertussis or tetanus vaccination on allergies and allergy-related respiratory symptoms among children and adolescents in the US. *Journal of Manipulative and Physiological Therapeutics* 318(7192):1173–76.

Jackson, D. J., R. E. Gangnon, M. D. Evans, K. A. Roberg, E. L. Anderson, T. E. Pappas, M. C. Printz, et al. 2008. Wheezing rhinovirus illnesses in early life predict asthma development in high-risk children. *American Journal of Respiratory and Critical Care Medicine* 178(7):667–72.

Karkos, P. D., and J. A. Wilson. 2006. Empiric treatment of laryngopharyngeal reflux with proton pump inhibitors: A systematic review. *Laryngoscope* 116(1):144–48.

Kelly, D., and A. G. Coutts. 2000. Early nutrition and the development of immune function in the neonate. *Proceedings of the Nutrition Society* 59(2):177–85.

Kelly, G. S. 1999. Larch arabinogalactan: Clinical relevance of a novel immune-enhancing polysaccharide. *Alternative Medicine Review* 4(2):96–103.

Kidd, P. 2003. Th1/Th2 balance: The hypothesis, its limitations, and implications for health and disease. *Alternative Medicine Review* (8)3:223–46.

Kolb, H., and P. Pozzilli. 1999. Cow's milk and type I diabetes: The gut immune system deserves attention. *Immunology Today* 20(3):108–10.

Krieger, J. W., L. Song, T. K. Takaro, and J. Stout. 2000. Asthma and the home environment of low-income urban children: Preliminary findings from the Seattle-King County healthy homes project. *Journal of Urban Health* 77(1):50-67.

Larson, A. M., J. Polson, R. J. Fontana, T. J. Davern, E. Lalani, L. S. Hynan, J. S. Reisch, et al. 2005. Acetaminophen-induced acute liver failure: Results of a United States multicenter, prospective study. *Hepatology* 42(6):1364–72.

Lee, J., D. Seto, and L. Bielory. 2008. Meta-analysis of clinical trials of probiotics for prevention and treatment of pediatric atopic dermatitis. *Journal of Allergy and Clinical Immunology* 121(1):116–21.

Lee, Y. K., K. Y. Puong, A. C. Ouwehand, and S. Salminen. 2003. Displacement of bacterial pathogens from mucus and Caco-2 cell surface by lactobacilli. *Journal of Medical Microbiology* 52(Pt 10):925–30.

Lucassen, P. L., W. J. Assendelft, J. W. Gubbels, A. K. Neven, J. T. M. Van Eijk, and W. J. Van Geldrop. 1998. Effectiveness of treatments for infantile colic: Systematic review. *British Medical Journal* 316(7144):1563–69.

Matsuoka, L. Y., J. Wortsman, J. G. Haddad, P. Kolm, and B. W. Hollis 1991. Racial pigmentation and the cutaneous synthesis of vitamin D. *Archives of Dermatology* 127(4):536–38.

Mattsby-Baltzer, I., A. Roseanu, C. Motas, J. Elverfors, I. Engberg, and L. A. Hanson. 1996. Lactoferrin or a fragment thereof inhibits the endotoxin-induced interleukin-6 response in human monocytic cells. *Pediatric Research* 40(2):257–62.

Mermer, C., and J. Mercola. 2002. Omega-3s and childhood asthma. [Letter to the editor.] *Thorax* 57(3):281.

Metcalf, T. J., T. G. Irons, L. D. Sher, and P. C. Young. 1994. Simethicone in the treatment of infant colic: A randomized, placebo-controlled, multicenter trial. *Pediatrics* 94(1):29–34.

Milgrom, H., D. P. Skoner, G. Bensch, K. T. Kim, R. Claus, and R. A. Baumgartner. 2001. Low-dose levalbuterol in children with asthma: Safety and efficacy in comparison with placebo and racemic albuterol. *Journal of Allergy and Clinical Immunology* 108(6):938–45.

Mössinger, P. 1985. Zur behandlung der otitis media mit *Pulsatilla*. *Kinderarzt* 16(4):581-82.

Morgan, J., P. Williams, F. Norris, C. M. Williams, M. Larkin, and S. Hampton. 2004. Eczema and early solid feeding in preterm infants. *Archives of Disease in Childhood* 89(4):309–14.

National Institute of Neurological Disorders and Stroke. 2009. Febrile seizures fact sheet. www.ninds.nih.gov/disorders/febrile_seizures/detail_febrile_seizures.htm. Accessed September 6, 2009.

Nelson, S. P., E. H. Chen, G. M. Syniar, K. K. Christoffel. 1997. Prevalence of gastroesophageal reflux during infancy. *Archives of Pediatric and Adolescent Medicine* 151(6): 569–572.

Neustaedter, R. 2005. *Child Health Guide: Holistic Pediatrics for Parents.* Berkeley, CA: North Atlantic Books.

———. 2002. *The Vaccine Guide: Risks and Benefits for Children and Adults.* Berkeley, CA: North Atlantic Books.

Nicholas, S. W., B. Jean-Louis, B. Ortiz, M. Northridge, K. Shoemaker, R. Vaughan, M. Rome, G. Canada, and V. Hutchinson. 2005. Addressing the childhood asthma crisis in Harlem: The Harlem Children's Zone Asthma Initiative. *American Journal of Public Health* 95(2):245–49.

Oddy, W. H., P. G. Holt, P. D. Sly, A. W. Read, L. I. Landau, F. J. Stanley, G. E. Kendall, and P. R. Burton. 1999. Association between breast feeding and asthma in 6 year old children: Findings of a prospective birth cohort study. *British Medical Journal* 319(7213):815–19.

Odent, M. R., E. E. Culpin, and T. Kimmel. 1994. Letter to the editor. Pertussis vaccination and asthma: Is there a link? *Journal of the American Medical Association* 272(8):592–93.

Ohm, J. 2009 Personal communication.

Oishi S. 2002. Effects of propyl paraben on the male reproductive system. *Food chemistry and toxicology* 40(12):1807–13.

Okamoto, M., F. Mitsunobu, K. Ashida, T. Mifune, T. Hosaki, H. Tsugeno, S. Harada, et al. 2000. Effects of perilla seed oil supplementation on leukotriene generation by leucocytes in patients with asthma associated with lipometabolism. *International Archives of Allergy and Immunology* 122(2):137–42.

Olafsdottir, E., S. Forshei, G. Fluge, and T. Markestad. 2001. Randomised controlled trial of infantile colic treated with chiropractic spinal manipulation. *Archives of Disease in Childhood* 84(2):138–41.

Orenstein, S. R., E. Hassall, W. Furmaga-Jablonska, S. Atkinson, and M. G. Raanan. 2009. Multicenter, double-blind, randomized, placebo-controlled trial assessing the efficacy and safety of proton pump inhibitor lansoprazole in infants with symptoms of gastroesophageal reflux disease. *Journal of Pediatrics* 154(4):514–20

Ouwehand, A., G. Leyer, and D. Carcano. 2008. Probiotics reduce incidence and duration of respiratory tract infection symptoms in 3- to 5-year-old children. *Pediatrics* 121(1, issue suppl.):115.

Paradise, J. L., C. D. Bluestone, K. D. Rogers, F. H. Taylor, D. K. Colborn, R. Z. Bachman, B. S. Bernard, and R. H. Schwarzbach. 1990. Efficacy of adenoidectomy for recurrent otitis media in children previously treated with tympanostomy-tube placement: Results of parallel randomized and nonrandomized trials. *Journal of the American Medical Association* 263(15):2066–73.

Patzelt-Wenczler, R., and E. Ponce-Poschl. 2000. Proof of efficacy of Kamillosan (R) cream in atopic eczema. *European Journal of Medical Research* 5(4):171–75.

Paul, I. A., K. E. Yoder, K. R. Crowell, M. L. Shaffer, H. S. McMillan, L. C. Carlson, D. A. Dilworth, and C. M. Berlin. 2004. Effect of dextromethorphan, diphenhydramine, and placebo on nocturnal cough and sleep quality for coughing children and their parents. *Pediatrics* 114(1):e85–90.

Plaisance, K. I., S. Kudaravalli, S. S. Wasserman, M. M. Levine, and P. A. Mackowiak. 2000. Effect of antipyretic therapy on the duration of illness in experimental influenza A, *Shigella sonnei*, and *Rickettsia rickettsii* infections. *Pharmacotherapy* 20(12):1417–22.

Rakes, G. P., E. Arruda, J. M. Ingram, G. E. Hoover, J. C. Zambrano, F. G. Hayden, T. Platts-Mills, and P. W. Heymann. 1999. Rhinovirus and respiratory syncytial virus in wheezing children requiring emergency care. *American Journal of Respiratory Critical Care Medicine* 159(3):785–90.

Rapelanoro, R., P. Mortureux, B. Couprie, J. Maleville, and A. Taieb. 1996. Neonatal *Malassezia furfur* pustulosis. *Archives of Dermatology* 132(2):190–93.

Ribeiro, H., and J. A. Vanderhoof. 1998. Reduction of diarrheal illness following administration of *Lactobacillus plantarum* 299v in a daycare facility. *Journal of Pediatric Gastroenterology and Nutrition* 265(5):561.

Rimsza, M. E., and S. Newberry. 2008. Unexpected infant deaths associated with use of cough and cold medications. *Pediatrics* 122(2):e318–22.

Rosenfeld, R. M., and D. Kay. 2003. Natural history of untreated otitis media. In *Evidence-Based Otitis Media* (2nd ed.), ed. R. M. Rosenfeld and C. D. Bluestone. Hamilton, ON, Canada: BC Decker.

Rosenfeldt, V., E. Benfeldt, S. D. Nielsen, K. F. Michaelsen, D. L. Jeppesen, N. H. Valerius, and A. Paerregaard. 2003. Effect of probiotic *Lactobacillus* strains in children with atopic dermatitis. *Journal of Allergy and Clinical Immunology* 111(2):389–95.

Rosenfeldt, V., E. Benfeldt, N. H. Valerius, A. Paerregaard, and K. Michaelsen. 2004. Effect of probiotics on gastrointestinal symptoms and small intestinal permeability in children with atopic dermatitis. *Journal of Pediatrics* 145(5):612–16.

Roydhouse, N. 1980. Adenoidectomy for otitis media with mucoid effusion. *Annals of Otology, Rhinology, and Laryngology. Supplement* 89(3 pt. 2):312–15.

Saarinen, U. M., and M. Kajosaari. 1995. Breastfeeding as prophylaxis against atopic disease: Prospective follow-up study until 17 years old. *Lancet* 346(8982):1065–69.

Salam, M. T., Y. Li, B. Langholz, and F. D. Gilliland. 2004. Early-life environmental risk factors for asthma: Findings from the Children's Health Study. *Environmental Health* 112(6):760–65.

Savino, F., E. Pelle, E. Palumeri, R. Oggero, and R. Miniero. 2007. *Lactobacillus reuteri* (American Type Culture Collection Strain 55730) versus simethicone in the treatment of infantile colic: A prospective randomized study. *Pediatrics* 119(1):e124-30.

Sharek, P. J., and D. A. Bergman. 2000. The effect of inhaled steroids on the linear growth of children with asthma: A meta-analysis. *Pediatrics* 106(1):e8.

Szajewska, H., and J. Z. Mrukowicz. 2001. Probiotics in the treatment and prevention of acute infectious diarrhea in infants and children: A systematic review of published randomized, double-blind, placebo-controlled trials. *Journal of Pediatric Gastroenterology and Nutrition* 33(suppl. 2):17–25.

Tollesson, A., and A. Frithz. 1993. Borage oil, an effective new treatment for infantile seborrheic dermatitis. *British Journal of Dermatology* 129(1):95.

Tollesson, A., A. Frithz, A. Berg, and G. Karlman. 1993. Essential fatty acids in infantile seborrheic dermatitis. *Journal of the American Academy of Dermatology* 28(6):957–61.

U.S. Food and Drug Administration. 2005. Public health advisory for Elidel and Protopic. www.fda.gov/Drugs/DrugSafety/PostmarketDrugSafetyInformationforPatientsandProviders/ucm153956.htm. Accessed September 6, 2009.

Van Gool, C., C. Thijs, C. Henquet, A. C. Van Houwelingen, P. C. Dagnelie, J. Schrander, P. P. Menheere, and P. A. Van Den Brandt. 2003. Gamma-linolenic acid supplementation for prophylaxis of atopic dermatitis: A randomized, controlled trial in infants at high familial risk. *American Journal of Clinical Nutrition* 77(4):943–51.

Van Sleuwen, B., M. L'Hoir, A. Engelberts, W. Busschers, P. Westers, M. Blom, T. Schulpen, and W. Kuis. 2006. Comparison of behavior modification with and without swaddling as interventions for excessive crying. *Journal of Pediatrics* 149(4):512–17.

Vardy, D. A., A. D. Cohen, T. Tchetov, E. Medvedovsky, and A. Biton. 1999. A double-blind, placebo-controlled trial of an Aloe vera (*A. barbadensis*) emulsion in the treatment of seborrheic dermatitis. *Journal of Dermatological Treatment* 10(1):7–11.

Vartabedian, B. 2007. *Colic Solved: The Essential Guide to Infant Reflux and the Care of Your Crying, Difficult-to-Soothe Baby.* New York: Ballantine Books.

Von Ehrenstein, O. S., E. Von Mutius, S. Illi, L. Baumann, O. Böhm, and R. Von Kries. 2000. Reduced risk of hay fever and asthma among children of farmers. *Clinical and Experimental Allergy* 30(2):187–93.

Wang, Y., C. B. Harvey, E. Hollox, A. Phillips, M. Poulter, P. Clay, J. Walker-Smith, and D. Swallow. 1998. The genetically programmed down-regulation of lactase in children. *Gastroenterology* 114(6):1230–36.

Weizman, Z., S. Alkrinawi, D. Goldfarb, and C. Bitran. 1993. Efficacy of herbal tea preparation in infantile colic. *Journal of Pediatrics* 122(4):650–52.

Weizman, Z., G. Asli, and A. Alsheikh. 2005. Effect of a probiotic infant formula on infections in child care centers: Comparison of two probiotic agents. *Pediatrics* 115(1):5–9.

Wickens, K., D. Barry, A. Friezema, R. Rhodius, N. Bone, G. Purdie, and J. Crane. 2005. Fast foods: Are they a risk factor for asthma? *Allergy* 60(12):1537–41.

Wickens, K., P. N. Black, T. Stanley, E. Mitchell, P. Fitzharris, G. Tannock, G. Purdie, and J. Crane. 2008. A differential effect of two probiotics in the prevention of eczema and atopy: A double-blind, randomized, placebo-controlled trial. *Journal of Allergy and Clinical Immunology* 122(4):788–94.

Widemar, L., C. Svensson, B. Rynnel-Dagoo, and H. Schiratzki. 1985. The effect of adenoidectomy on secretory otitis media: A 2-year controlled prospective study. *Clinical Otolaryngology and Allied Sciences* 10(6):345–50.

Randall Neustaedter, OMD, has practiced and taught holistic medicine for more than thirty years in the San Francisco Bay area, specializing in child health care. He is a licensed acupuncturist and doctor of Chinese medicine, author of *Child Health Guide* and *The Vaccine Guide*, and the father of five children. Visit his website, www.cure-guide.com, to register for a free newsletter with pediatric updates

index

Also by Randall Neustaedter: *Child Health Guide*

Child Health Guide: Holistic Pediatrics for Parents
By Randall Neustaedter
978-1-55643-564-5, $17.95

Child Health Guide respects parents' choices while providing
persuasive arguments for building a healthy immune system by
avoiding conventional drugs and stressing natural methods. Using an
educational and informative tone, the book discusses preventive
medicine, the causes of poor health in children, and common foods and
chemical exposures that can contribute to chronic illness.

Available at NorthAtlanticBooks.com

more books from newharbingerpublications, inc.

MINDFUL MOTHERHOOD

Practical Tools for Staying
Sane During Pregnancy &
Your Child's First Year

US $16.95 / ISBN: 978-1572246294
Copublished with Noetic Books
Also available as an **eBook**
at **newharbinger.com**

**MORE VEGETABLES,
PLEASE!**

Over 100 Easy & Delicious
Recipes for Eating Healthy
Foods Each & Every Day

US $21.95 / ISBN: 978-1572245907

**BREASTFEEDING MADE
SIMPLE**

Seven Natural Laws for
Nursing Mothers

US $16.95 / ISBN: 978-1572244047
Also available as an **eBook**
at **newharbinger.com**

**THE BABY EMERGENCY
HANDBOOK**

Lifesaving Information Every
Parent Needs to Know

US $14.95 / ISBN: 978-1572245662

THE BALANCED MOM

Raising Your Kids
Without Losing Your Self

US $14.95 / ISBN: 978-1572244535

THE JOY OF PARENTING

An Acceptance & Commitment
Therapy Guide to Effective
Parenting in the Early Years

US $17.95 / ISBN: 978-1572245938

available from

newharbingerpublications, inc.

and fine booksellers everywhere

To order, call toll free **1-800-748-6273**

or visit our online bookstore at **www.newharbinger.com**

(VISA, MC, AMEX / prices subject to change without notice)

Sign up for our Book Alerts
at newharbinger.com

31901050620121